C. P. CAVAFY: SELECTED POEMS

CONSTANTINE P. CAVAFY, the youngest of seven brothers, was born in 1863, in Alexandria, Egypt. Both his parents came from well-off merchant families in Constantinople (modern Istanbul). His father, Peter Cavafy, who held both Greek and British citizenship, had set up offices of the family import/export firm in England before establishing one in Alexandria and settling his family there in 1855. Not long after Peter Cavafy's death in 1870, the surviving family members moved to England, where Constantine spent much of his adolescence. The influence of this sojourn in Albion was profound: his earliest poetry was in English and both his poetic oeuvre and his prose criticism demonstrate deep conversance with the English poetic tradition. Cavafy spent the remainder of his life, apart from one other interval (from 1882 to 1885), in Alexandria, which he rarely left. After showing early interest in journalism as a career, he later found work as a clerk at the Ministry of Public Works, where he stayed until his retirement in 1922. Cavafy lived a relatively unremarkable, not to say cloistered, public life. E. M. Forster, who met him in Alexandria in 1916, commented that he only saw him 'going either from his flat to the office or from his office to the flat'. This existence on the quiet fringe of things would characterize so much in his life: he was a Greek poet living outside of Greece writing in a diaspora Greek outpost; his meticulously crafted and understated verse was the antithesis of the jingoistic paeans popular in Athens at the time; and of course, the homosexual background of his love poems could hardly be called mainstream. Cavafy never published a collection in book form, preferring to issue his poems in newspapers or periodicals, and then printing them privately in individual sheets which he would assemble into makeshift collections for visitors or other interested parties. The first volume of 154 poems, which constitute his poetic canon, was published posthumously in Alexandria. Ironist, cosmopolitan and decadent, Cavafy's stoic, sage-like voice would appeal to an increasingly broad readership over time, including many non-Greeks. Among the very first of these was Forster. From there the literary fan club would expand to comprise a veritable *Who's Who* of English and American poets and writers, including T. E. Lawrence, Lawrence Durrell, W. H. Auden, John Fowles, James Merrill and many others. He died in 1933.

AVI SHARON works on Wall Street and lives in Brooklyn with his wife and two sons. He holds a PhD in Classics from Boston University and taught in Athens and the US before leaving academia. He has written widely on Greek topics, ancient and modern, and has translated a variety of poets and others writers, including George Seferis, Odysseas Elytis, Eugenio Montale, Haim Gouri and others. His translation of Plato's *Symposium* came out in 1998.

C. P. CAVAFY

Selected Poems

Translated with an introduction by AVI SHARON

PENGUIN BOOKS

PENGUIN CLASSICS

Published by the Penguin Group
Penguin Books Ltd, 80 Strand, London WC2R ORL, England
Penguin Group (USA) Inc., 375 Hudson Street, New York, New York 10014, USA
Penguin Group (Canada), 90 Eglinton Avenue East, Suite 700, Toronto, Ontario, Canada M4P 2Y3
(a division of Pearson Penguin Canada Inc.)
Penguin Ireland, 25 St Stephen's Green, Dublin 2, Ireland
(a division of Penguin Books Ltd)
Penguin Group (Australia), 250 Camberwell Road, Camberwell, Victoria 3124, Australia
(a division of Pearson Australia Group Pty Ltd)
Penguin Books India Pvt Ltd, 11 Community Centre, Panchsheel Park, New Delhi – 110 017, India
Penguin Group (NZ), 67 Apollo Drive, Rosedale, North Shore 0632, New Zealand
(a division of Pearson New Zealand Ltd)
Penguin Books (South Africa) (Pty) Ltd, 24 Sturdee Avenue, Rosebank, Johannesburg 2196, South Africa

Penguin Books Ltd, Registered Offices: 80 Strand, London WC2R ORL, England

www.penguin.com

First published 2008

017

Translation and editorial material copyright © Avi Sharon, 2008
All rights reserved

The moral right of the translator and editor has been asserted

Set in 10.25/12.25pt PostScript Adobe Sabon
Typeset by Rowland Phototypesetting Ltd, Bury St Edmunds, Suffolk
Printed and bound in Great Britain by Clays Ltd, Elcograf S.p.A.

ISBN: 978-0-141-18561-3

www.greenpenguin.co.uk

Contents

Part I: Poems 1897–1904

Part II: Poems 1905–1915

Part III: Poems 1916–1918

Part IV: Poems 1919–1933

CONTENTS ix

Chronology

1863 (*29 April*) Constantine Petrou Photiades Cavafy is born in Alexandria, Egypt (then under Ottoman rule), the youngest of seven brothers, to Peter John Cavafy, a successful merchant, and Charicleia Photiades.

1870 C.'s father dies, precipitating a decline in the family's fortunes.

1872 At nine years of age, C. moves to England with his family, settling first in Liverpool, then in London. Earlier, Peter Cavafy had established offices of the family firm, Cavafy & Co., in both locations, as well as in Manchester, Constantinople and Alexandria.

1876 Cavafy & Co. is dissolved; Charicleia and her children return to Alexandria in the following year, settling in a modest apartment.

1878 C. attends the Hermes School in Alexandria to study business.

1882 Local unrest (culminating in the British bombardment of the city) inclines Charicleia to travel with her youngest son to Constantinople; date of C.'s first surviving poem in manuscript, 'Leaving Therapia', written in English.

1885 C. returns to Alexandria; joint British and Ottoman rule imposed in Egypt; C. renounces his British citizenship.

1886 Begins to publish poems and essays in several Alexandrian literary magazines; in Alexandria, C. lives with his mother and his brothers Paul and John, the closest to him in age.

1891 C.'s brother Peter dies, inaugurating a series of losses in the family that include his mother in 1899, in 1900 his brother George, in 1902 his brother Aristeides and in 1905 his brother Alexander.

1892 Finds work in the Ministry of Public Works as a temporary clerk – his Greek citizenship excluded him from a permanent position at the colonial-run agency; he continues to hold this temporary position (renewed annually) for thirty years.

1899 C.'s mother dies; he continues to live with his two brothers, Paul and John, until 1904, when John moves to Cairo.

1907 C. and Paul move to an apartment on rue Lepsius; C. later offered a telling gloss on the suitability of this Alexandrian residence: 'Where could I live better? Under me is a house of ill repute, which caters to the needs of the flesh. Over there is the church, where sins are forgiven. And beyond is the hospital, where we die.'

1908 Paul travels abroad, never to return; C., at the age of forty-five, begins to live on his own for the first time.

1916 Makes the acquaintance of E. M. Forster (in Alexandria working for the Red Cross); Forster mentions C. in his *Alexandria: A History and a Guide*, published in 1922. A separate essay on C. appears in Forster's *Pharos and Pharillon* (1923).

1922 Retires from thirty-year career in the Ministry of Public Works.

1933 (29 April) C. dies, seventy years old to the day.

1948 The first collection of the 154 poems that comprise C.'s poetic canon is published posthumously in Greece.

1951 The first full volume of C.'s poems in English is published, translated by John Mavrogordato.

Introduction

Long before word of his poetry had spread beyond a relatively narrow circle of readers in Alexandria and Athens, the Greek poet Constantine P. Cavafy vaunted that, in time, he would acquire an audience both sizeable and discriminating:

> Cavafy, in my opinion, is an ultra-modern poet, a writer destined for future generations. For in addition to the historical, psychological and philosophical qualities of his verse, there is the sobriety of his impeccable manner, bordering on the laconic, his poised enthusiasm which elicits a form of cerebral emotion, his mastery of phrasing the result of his aristocratic ease, and the light touch of his irony – all elements that will hold greater appeal for future readers . . . [1]

The observations, conveyed in a mix of braggadocio and self-mockery so familiar from his many poetic impersonations, are both acute (about the poetry) and prescient (about the outcome), particularly for those readers who happened also to be poets. W. H. Auden, who was among the earlier non-Greek champions of Cavafy's work, wrote of the poet's 'unique tone of voice'. Joseph Brodsky later characterized the poet's vocal qualities in language that recalls Cavafy's mock commentary, as a 'hedonistic-stoic tremolo'.[2] In point of fact, of Cavafy's many Anglo-American admirers, only E. M. Forster experienced the poet's voice first hand, having befriended him in pre-war Alexandria. Nevertheless, Lawrence Durrell, James Merrill, Derek Mahon and others would come to regard Cavafy's voice, even when heard through translation, as one of the most singular, poignant and *imitable* in twentieth-century European poetry.

Imitation, arguably, is the sincerest indication of esteem. On that score, Cavafy's verse ranks high, as it has had an indisputably creative influence on the world's poets (including Auden, Czesław Miłosz and James Merrill) and novelists (among them, Forster, Durrell and Marguerite Yourcenar).[3] By another measure of renown, several of his poems (such as 'Ithaca' or 'Waiting for the Barbarians') are among the most recognized titles in the literary marketplace. Such high and broad praise for any Greek poet is rare, but in the case of Cavafy it is downright remarkable given the man's painfully reclusive character, his writing in a marginal Egyptian city in a marginalized modern Greek tongue, and his scrupulously controlled method of distributing his poetry among select friends and associates in pamphlets of his own making.

But as he himself forecast, word would eventually out: nearly twenty years after Cavafy's death (in 1933) the first full volume of his poems appeared in English, enabling the tardy discovery of Cavafy by Anglo-American readers as a universal poet and proto-modernist, in the mould of a Brecht, Kafka or Borges. Suddenly Cavafy was seen to have written, along the lines of Eliot's thinking, with the tradition in his bones, leveraging themes and appropriating lines from Homer, Callimachus, Dante, Shakespeare and Browning. Cavafy likewise had employed a dogged 'correlative', his ramifying metaphor a decaying Alexandria, the city whose decline reflected in large the poet's own. Throughout his poetry, lyrical evocations of his remembered (and illicit, because homosexual) passions are cunningly interleaved with the historical-dramatic records of the Hellenistic city's (and greater Hellenism's) fabulous past, creating a single mythos encompassing both personal and collective memory. This world of his creation, Cavafy's unreal city, would be seen to rival in variety and richness Joyce's Dublin, Eliot's London or Pound's more extravagant commonwealth of *The Cantos*.

Yet of this beautiful and curious world there is little evidence in Cavafy's personal history. He was born Constantine Peter

Cavafy, on 29 April 1863, in Alexandria, the youngest of seven children (two elder siblings, a boy and the sole girl, died in infancy). Both parents, Peter John Cavafy and Charicleia Photiades, came from well-off merchant families in Constantinople. The two had migrated to Alexandria to establish the Egypt branch of Cavafy & Co., an import/export firm that already included offices in Liverpool, Manchester and London. But by the time his father died in 1870, the family business was on the wane. Two years later, his mother took the family to England, where they remained for about five years, returning to Alexandria in 1877, a year after the firm was dissolved. Cavafy, who was by now fifteen, enrolled in a trade school to study business (he had previously been home-tutored in both French and English), but xenophobic and anti-Christian hostilities broke out in Alexandria in the summer of 1882, prompting Charicleia to seek safe harbour for herself and Constantine among extended family in Constantinople for the next few years.

After returning to Alexandria in 1885, Constantine went to work as a provisional clerk in the Third Circle of Irrigation of the Ministry of Public Works ('provisional' because, having renounced his British citizenship in favour of his Greek one, he could not be offered a permanent position at the colonial-run ministry). He continued to work there for thirty years, retiring in 1922. Until his mother's death in 1899, he lived with her, and then with his brothers John, who moved to Cairo in 1904, and Paul, who left for Paris in 1908. Alone for the first time in his life, Cavafy settled at 10 rue Lepsis, where he remained until his death, on his seventieth birthday, in 1933.

The fact that his biography offers only a flash or two of relevance to the student of his poetry should not surprise. The world that Cavafy describes in his verse is an interior one, one created by and accessible through the imagination. Indeed, in an early *ars poetica* he wrote that the notion that a writer derives most profit from 'personal experience is undoubtedly a sound one; but were it strictly observed it would limit tremendously literary production'.[4] Cavafy's literary production – snapshots of remembered affairs, retellings of historical

passages, imagined monologues – may have had its beginning
in spontaneous and powerful feelings, but the poems make
clear (sometimes explicitly) that they were recollected in tran-
quillity, and later preserved within the polished amber of his
verse, as in 'Their Beginning':

> The fulfilling of their lawless pleasures
> now complete, they rise from the bed
> and hurriedly dress without speaking.
> They emerge separately, furtively from the house,
> and as they walk somewhat uneasily down the street,
> it appears they suspect something about them betrays
> the sort of bed they fell upon just a moment ago.
>
> But what great profit to the artist's life:
> tomorrow, the day after, or years later, he'll write
> the powerful lines that had their beginning here.

As one preternaturally disposed to look both within and
beyond his own experience, sifting through both individual
and tribal memory for the material of his verse – visiting cities
of the Hellenistic diaspora, arguing details of a scene from
Plutarch's Alexandria or Gibbon's Constantinople, reviving
passions of old and recent date – he may have felt the need,
at times, to remind himself where imagination ended and his
own reality began, as exemplified by 'Morning Sea':

> Let me stop right here. Let me, too, have a look at nature:
> the morning sea and the cloudless sky,
> both a luminous blue, the yellow shore, all of it
> beautiful, and in such magnificent light.
>
> Let me stop right here. Let me pretend this is actually
> what I'm seeing (I really did see it, when I first stopped)
> and not, here too, more of those fantasies of mine,
> more of those memories, those voluptuous illusions.

This is hardly the confession of a landscape poet or of one with much interest in light or colour (on the contrary, interiors, walls and shadows frame most of Cavafy's poems). In fact, the image of the poet in these lines recalls a remark of Forster's in which the visiting Englishman described Cavafy as 'a Greek gentleman in a straw hat, standing absolutely motionless at an angle to the universe'.[5] The vision of the poet at such an oblique angle to the world is sometimes interpreted as a gloss on his marginality, his difference and distance from the mainstream – whether in geographic, sexual or literary terms. Others connect it to the strong current of irony, the feel of detached observation, that runs through nearly all of Cavafy's work. The anecdote is deservedly famous, and points suggestively toward a fundamental truth about the man, something that endows Cavafy's verse with its singular quality of honesty and insight.

This quality, the poet's essential wisdom, is captured in another comment from his poetic credo: 'a state of feeling is true and false, possible and impossible at the same time or rather by turns'. This ingrained ironic perspective (an awareness of 'the inherent contradiction in every human utterance')[6] evolved in Cavafy a verse form that could naturally accommodate it, a version of Browning's dramatic monologue, but one that permits a crack in the fourth wall for occasional authorial voice-over, as in 'Of the Jews, AD 50':

> Painter and poet, sprinter and discus-thrower,
> with Endymion's beauty, Ianthes, son of Antony,
> of a family dear to the Synagogue:
>
> 'My proudest days are those
> when I leave behind all sensuous pursuits,
> when I abandon hard, beautiful Hellenism,
> with its sovereign ideal
> of perfectly formed and perishable white limbs,
> and I become that which I hope
> forever to remain: a son of the Jews, of the Holy Jews.'

> Too fervent, his confession: 'Forever to remain
> of the Jews, of the Holy Jews . . .'
>
> He didn't remain that at all.
> Pleasure and the fine arts of Alexandria
> kept him their passionate disciple.

If the young man's confession were not understood to be a bit
fulsome, the poet clears the air with a concluding counter: 'But
he didn't remain that at all.' This tendency to probe beneath
the adamant veneer, to look at the world from an angle of
querying repose, is something the poet applies to most of the
personae, imagined or real, named or anonymous, within his
diverse poetic troupe. Take 'He Vows':

> Every now and then   he vows to live a better life.
> But when night comes   with her own counsels,
> with her promises   and her compromises,
> when night comes   with her power
> over the body   that seeks and yearns,
> he returns, lost,   to the same fatal pleasures.

On occasion the ironic slant can be more reticent in convey-
ing its contrary view. This often occurs when Cavafy is en-
gaging in creative argument with one of the historical sources
upon which a poem turns. In one example ('Of Coloured
Glass'), he takes issue with Gibbon's characterization of the
increasingly dire straits of the Byzantine throne. The poem was
inspired by the ceremony in 1347 that combined the crowning
of John Cantacuzenus as emperor with the wedding of his
daughter Helen to John V Palaeologus. Gibbon, in his *Decline
and Fall*, describes the affair in a condescending tone, referring
to the royal jewels as 'paltry artifices':

The festival of the coronation and nuptials was celebrated with
the appearances of concord and magnificence, and both were
equally fallacious. During the late troubles, the treasures of the
state, and even the furniture of the palace, had been alienated or

embezzled; the royal banquet was served in pewter or earthen-
ware; and such was the proud poverty of the times, that the
absence of gold and jewels was supplied by the paltry artifices of
glass and gilt-leather.

Cavafy, in proud contrast, sees the impromptu substitution
of coloured glass for the crown jewels as neither 'base' nor
'undignified'. Rather, he finds that the ersatz shards convey
a heartfelt and justifiable lament over the erstwhile glory of
Byzantium:

> I am quite touched by one detail
> in the coronation, at Blachernai, of John Cantacuzenus
> and Irene, daughter of Andronicus Asan.
> Because they had only a few precious stones
> (the poverty of our wretched kingdom being so great)
> they wore artificial gems: hundreds of pieces made of glass,
> red, green and blue. There is nothing
> base or undignified, in my view,
> about these little bits
> of coloured glass. On the contrary, they seem
> like a sorrowful protest
> against the undeserved misfortunes of the crown.
> They are the symbols of what should have been worn,
> of what, assuredly, ought to have been worn
> at the coronation of Lord John Cantacuzenus
> and his Lady Irene, daughter of Andronicus Asan.

The sorrowful protest here is shared by Cavafy and directed
against the judgement of Gibbon, who certainly showed
himself to be no fan of Greek Byzantium in his record of
Roman decline. It was a minor point, but Cavafy chose to
rescue this otherwise forgettable detail to offer a corrective,
more sympathetic view.

Sympathy sometimes requires the suppression, or at least the
suspension, of irony, and there are many examples of Cavafy's
engagement with history where fellow-feeling, not detached
criticism, is the dominant tone. In the poem 'Caesarion', in

which his poetic process is made largely transparent, Cavafy illustrates the manner in which he brings to life, at the touch of a page, some remote and nearly forgotten episode:

> In part to verify a date,
> and in part just to pass the time,
> last night I picked up a volume
> of Ptolemaic inscriptions and began reading.
> [. . .]
>
> When I managed to find the date in question,
> I'd have put the book aside had a brief mention
> of King Caesarion, an insignificant note really,
> not suddenly caught my eye . . .
>
> Ah, there you stood, with that vague
> charm of yours. And since history has devoted
> just a few lines to you, I had more freedom
> to fashion you in my mind's eye . . .
> I made you handsome, capable of deep feeling.
> My art gave your face an appealing,
> dreamlike beauty. In fact, I imagined you
> so vividly last night, that when my lamp
> went out – I let it go out on purpose –
> I actually thought you had come into my room;
> you were there, standing before me,
> just as you would have looked in defeated Alexandria,
> pale and tired, ideal in your sorrow,
> still hoping for mercy from those vicious men
> who kept on whispering 'too many Caesars'.

Cavafy had a knack for discovering in old annals, tombstones and other less heralded detritus, the material out of which his poetry grew. In Cavafy's poetic conversation with the past (as in 'Voices', quoted below), memory and imagination help unlock from their prisons these characters long lost to history:

Ideal voices, the beloved voices
of those who have died or of those who are
lost to us as if they were dead.

Sometimes they speak to us in dreams;
sometimes, in thought, the mind hears them.

And with their sounds for a moment return
sounds from our life's first poetry –
like music at night, far off, fading out.

And when they revive, it is his voice in theirs that we recognize.

NOTES

1. C. P. Cavafy, 'Sur le poète', in *Unpublished Prose Texts*, ed.
    M. Peridis (Ikaros, Athens, 1963). All translations from this
    work are by the translator of the current volume unless
    otherwise indicated.
2. W. H. Auden, 'Introduction', in *The Complete Poems of C. P.
    Cavafy*, translated by Rae Dalven (Harcourt Brace & World,
    New York, 1961), p. viii; Joseph Brodsky, *Less Than One:
    Selected Essays* (Farrar Straus & Giroux, New York, 1986),
    p. 67.
3. Most directly and visibly in *Pharos and Pharillon* by E. M.
    Forster (1923); *The Alexandria Quartet* by Lawrence Durrell
    (1957–60); James Merrill's 'Days of 1964' (1966); and several
    of Auden's poems, including 'Atlantis' (1941) and 'Rois
    Fainéants' (1968).
4. In *Unpublished Prose Texts*, pp. 82–4.
5. From 'The Poetry of C. P. Cavafy', in *Pharos and Pharillon* by
    E. M. Forster (Knopf, New York, 1923), pp. 91–2.
6. From the essay 'Philosophical Scrutiny', in *Unpublished Prose
    Texts*.

Further Reading

Arguably the finest guide to further reading about Cavafy and his poems is the poet himself. The composition of many of the poems was sparked by Cavafy's own critical reading, primarily of Hellenistic and Byzantine history, and quite often by the works of two authors: Plutarch (the *Lives*) and Gibbon (*The History of the Decline and Fall of the Roman Empire*). The individual poems frequently go out of their way to identify the source (in some cases by direct quotation) and bring to life a passage Cavafy either admired or sought to engage. By following the poet's own trail and exploring these works (the sources and individual passages are identified in the notes to this edition), the reader will gain direct insight into the impulse and argument behind much of the poetry.

Going beyond Cavafy's immediate sources, perhaps the richest vein of general commentary about the poet, and the most enjoyable to read, comes from admirers of his work who are themselves writers. This list begins with E. M. Forster ('The Poetry of C. P. Cavafy', in *Pharos and Pharillon*, Knopf, New York, 1923) and includes W. H. Auden ('Introduction', in *The Complete Poems of C. P. Cavafy*, translated by Rae Dalven, Harcourt Brace & World, New York, 1961), James Merrill ('Marvelous Poet', *The New York Review of Books*, 17 July 1975) and Joseph Brodsky (*Less Than One: Selected Essays*, Farrar Straus & Giroux, New York, 1986), among others. Peter Bien's *Constantine Cavafy* (Columbia University Press, New York, 1964) is an excellent introduction to the poet and his work. Meanwhile, a superb and concise study of the poet's tone, technique and metre is *C. P. Cavafy* (Bristol Classical Press, Bristol, 1988) by Christopher Robinson.

For those interested in the life behind the writing there is as yet no authoritative biography in English, the closest equivalent being Robert Liddell's *Cavafy: A Critical Biography* (Duckworth, London, 1974). Alternatively, there is Edmund Keeley's admirable literary biography, *Cavafy's Alexandria: Study of a Myth in Progress* (Harvard University Press, Cambridge, MA, 1976), and a recent recounting of the city that stood as his own muse (and that of others), *Alexandria, City of Memory* (Yale University Press, New Haven, CT, 2004) by Michael Haag.

Translator's Note

Poets generally give a good deal of thought to the order and publication of their finished work, and Cavafy is no exception. In fact, few poets show such concern over the minutiae of punctuation, layout, organization and the printing of their work as did Cavafy. It is ironic, then, that the many collections of his work that we possess today show so little consistency.

Cavafy's verse may be broadly divided into the poems that were published during his lifetime and those termed 'unpublished', and which were issued subsequent to his death. Cavafy labelled his unpublished poems either 'hidden' or 'unfinished' – each of them categories that suggest Cavafy would have preferred they remain under wraps. Among the 'published' poems there are again two groupings, the 'acknowledged' poems (which constitute the so-called 'canon' of 154 poems in this volume), and the 'repudiated' poems. Of this latter set we have emphatic indication from Cavafy himself that it had 'absolutely no relation to his current work and has been rejected by the author himself'.

While there may be agreement about the acknowledged or canonical poems, there is no authoritative consensus regarding their appropriate sequence. In the last years of his life, Cavafy had three privately printed collections of his poems in circulation. Two of them, *Poems 1905–1915* and *Poems 1916–1918*, were bound booklets with the poems arranged by theme. The third collection, *Poems 1919–1930*, contained poems arranged chronologically, in order of first publication. It was unbound and the pages were held together by a pin so that new poems could be added once they had been published.

The greatest confusion arises with regard to the earliest work and Cavafy's first collections. Between 1891 and 1904, Cavafy had experimented with the printing of his own poems in various pamphlet-like forms, but it was only in late 1904 that he commissioned a small booklet in an edition of 100 copies, called *Poems 1904*. This book, Cavafy's first proper collection, contained fourteen poems whose publication dates range from the earliest acknowledged poems (published in 1897) to those published in 1904. In 1910 Cavafy produced a second, enlarged edition that went by the title *Poems 1910*, with an additional seven poems (published or revised in the intervening years 1905–9) added to the original fourteen from the 1904 edition. This volume later evolved piecemeal into successive collections including the final 1905–15 collection. One consequence of this process is that there are a number of poems (six in fact, published from 1905 to 1909) that are included in both *Poems 1910* and *Poems 1905–1915*. In a compromise attempt to retain Cavafy's own organization of his work, I have chosen to keep both the 1904 edition (but for the inclusion of 'Walls', which was inserted at a later date, and 'The Funeral of Sarpedon', which was revised later but which Cavafy considered to be a poem of that early period) and the final 1905–15 edition more or less intact. As a result, the order of the poems in this translation is as follows:

Part I: Poems 1897–1904, including only those issued from 1897 to 1904, with the addition of 'Walls' and 'The Funeral of Sarpedon'

Part II: Poems 1905–1915, including the six poems issued between 1905 and 1909 that were reprinted from the 1910 edition – 'Monotony', 'Trojans', 'King Demetrius', 'The Procession of Dionysus', 'The Footsteps', 'That's the Man!'

Part III: Poems 1916–1918

Part IV: Poems 1919–1933

So much for the sequence and content of the four major collections that constitute the agreed-upon canon. However, within these four sections there was another sequential logic where two main organizational principles, chronology and theme, had to make their peace. By chronology, Cavafy meant the date of a poem's publication, usually in a local, Alexandrian literary journal. Regarding the question of theme, the poet himself provided a now famous guide: 'Cavafy has three areas of concern: the philosophical (or reflective), the historical and the erotic (or sensual).' Close analysis of the poems shows that in those collections that were organized by theme (all but the last), Cavafy's three categories, broadly understood, are kept relatively discrete. Take the 1905–15 collection as an example: the first group of 'philosophical' poems runs from 'The City' to 'As Much As You Can'; 'Trojans' to 'Manuel Comnenus' represent the 'historical' series (their sequence is dictated by the periods described in the poems themselves, from the Homeric up to the Byzantine era); and the poems between 'In Church' and 'Chandelier' make up the 'sensual' cluster.

Across and certainly within these groupings, there can be no doubt that Cavafy intended the poems to complement and comment on each other through their juxtaposition. For his was a work in progress where, as he put it, 'the light of a new poem could subtly penetrate the half-light of an older poem'. Consider the 'philosophical' section that opens the 1905–15 collection: a general sense of entrapment and paralysis, of the vanity of human life and effort, suffuses the entire movement. In addition, verbal links run from poem to poem, binding the character metaphysically trapped in 'The City' to the accomplished journeyman in 'The Satrapy' who, trapped in another sense, leaves for the eastern provinces only to discover he cannot find there what he most desires; from the wise men full of foresight in 'The Wise Perceive Imminent Events' to the uninformed and unlucky Caesar of 'The Ides of March' and the anxious populace unable to sidestep their own precipitous destiny in 'Done'; and so on, until finally, to close the circle, we return to the despairing Trojans pent up within their own doomed city.

While Auden thought that Cavafy used language simply and

Marguerite Yourcenar translated him into limpid French prose, the reality is that his Greek was a unique and austere alloy of legal diction, inscriptions on tombs, echoes from the *Greek* (or *Palatine*) *Anthology* and the Septuagint, all inflected by an urbane use of the vernacular or demotic Greek. Its richness and feel are simply impossible to wholly convey in English. In addition, as some of the earlier poems are rhymed and many of them have rather complex structures, it has been possible to retain only the general contours of these in many instances. The translations were made from the Greek edition of Cavafy's *Poems 1896–1933*, edited by G. P. Savidis (Ikaros, Athens, 1991).

PART I

POEMS 1897–1904

Voices

Ideal voices, the beloved voices
of those who have died or of those who are
lost to us as if they were dead.

Sometimes they speak to us in dreams;
sometimes, in thought, the mind hears them.

And with their sounds for a moment return
sounds from our life's first poetry –
like music at night, far off, fading out.

Desires

Like the beautiful bodies of those who died young,
tearfully interred in a grand mausoleum
with roses by their heads and jasmine at their feet –
so seem those desires that have passed
without fulfilment; without a single night
of pleasure, or one of its radiant mornings.

Candles

The days of the future stand before us
like a line of burning candles –
golden candles, warm with life.

Behind them stand the days of our past,
a pitiful row of candles extinguished,
the nearest still sending up their smoke:
cold and melted, withered sticks.

I don't want to look; their image makes me sad,
it saddens me to recall their kindling.
I look ahead at the ones still burning.

I don't want to turn and see, with horror,
how quickly the line of shadow lengthens,
how quickly the number of snuffed candles grows.

An Old Man

Deep in the back of the noisy café
an old man sits alone, bent over a table,
with his newspaper spread out before him.

He feels contempt for his miserable old age
and recalls how little he enjoyed the years
when he had strength, eloquence and beauty.

He knows he has aged; he feels it; he sees it.
And yet the time when he was young seems
like yesterday. How short a span! How short!

He recalls how Prudence kept deceiving him,
how he always listened when she lied to him, saying:
'Tomorrow. There's plenty of time.' What folly!

He counts up the desires he held back, the joys
he squandered; each forfeited delight
returning now to mock his senseless caution . . .

But with all the thinking and reminiscence
the old man grows dizzy. He falls asleep,
propped against the table in the back of the café.

Prayer

The sea's taken a sailor to her depths below –
his mother, still unaware, rushes to go

light a narrow candle before the Virgin's shrine,
for his swift return, good weather, or a sign

that she struggles against the wind to hear.
But as she bows and reiterates her prayer,

the icon listens, sorrowful and glum,
quite sure that her son will never come.

Old Men's Souls

Within their ancient, decrepit bodies
the souls of old men wallow.
Poor things, so full of sorrow:
how bored with the wretched life they bear,
yet how they cherish it and how they fear
its loss, these contrary and befuddled
souls, tragicomically huddled
inside their ancient, desiccated hides.

The First Step

Complaining to Theocritus one day
the young poet Eumenes said:
'It's two years now since I began to write
and I've finished just one idyll so far.
It's my only accomplished work to date.
I see now the ascent up the ladder
of Poetry is terribly steep and,
judging from my place here on this first step,
I don't think I'll ever manage the climb.'
Theocritus replied: 'Such language
is inappropriate, verging on outrage.
For though you stand merely on the ladder's first step
you should be proud and delighted with your success.
To arrive at that point is no small feat;
the work you have finished is a great achievement.
For having reached only that first step
sets you far apart from the general mob.
Just to set foot on this first step
you must already, in your own right,
be a citizen of the republic of ideas.
And it is a hard and rare thing
to be written into the roll-books there.
In the market of that city you will find Lawmakers
that no fortune-hunter can fool.
To arrive at that point is no small feat;
the work you have finished is a great achievement.'

Interruption

The work of the gods we ourselves interrupt,
hasty, naïve, creatures of a day.
In the palaces of Phthia and Eleusis
Thetis and Demeter begin their work
amid rising flames and impenetrable smoke. But then,
from the king's chambers, Metaneira appears,
hair undone, frozen in terror,
while Peleus, afraid, intervenes.

Thermopylae

Honour to those who in their lives
defined and defend a Thermopylae.
Never shunning their duty;
just and decent in all their affairs,
yet also given to pity and compassion;
generous when rich, and when poor
generous still, in small ways,
helping others as their resources permit;
always speaking the truth
yet without rancour for those who do not.

And greater honour still is owed those
who foresee (and many do)
that Ephialtes will appear in the end,
and the Medes will break through after all.

Che Fece ... Il Gran Rifiuto

To some people there will come a day
when they must speak the great No or great Yes.
Immediately it is clear who is avid to release
the Yes within him, and once he says it,

off he goes, confident in his answer and his honour.
The one who refuses will not change his mind.
Ask him again and again he'll decline;
yet that No – the correct No – condemns him forever.

The Windows

In these dark rooms where I pass
such listless days, I wander up and down
looking for the windows – when a window opens
there will be some relief.
But there are no windows, or at least
I cannot find them. And perhaps it's just as well.
Perhaps the light would prove another torment.
Who knows what new things it would reveal?

Walls

Without compunction, pity or shame,
they've built towering walls around me.

Desperate, I sit and think one thing:
alone here this fate confounds me.

For there were many things I'd hoped to do out there.
With all the construction, how was I not aware?

Yet the crack and clang of hammers I never once heard.
Imperceptibly they've confined me from the outside world.

Waiting for the Barbarians

What are we waiting for, all gathered in the forum?

    The barbarians are coming today.

Why is there such inertia in the Senate?
Why are the senators just sitting there, not passing laws?

    Because the barbarians are coming today.
    What laws should the senators pass now?
    When the barbarians come they'll draft our laws.

Why is the emperor out of bed so early?
Why is he sitting at the city's main gate,
crowned and looking so formal on his throne?

    Because the barbarians are coming today
    and the emperor is arranging a welcome
    for their leader. In fact, he has prepared
    a formal decree, and on the parchment
    he has written numerous titles and marks of respect.

Why have our two consuls and praetors come out today,
dressed in their embroidered red togas?
Why are they wearing bracelets set with amethysts,
and rings with bright, shining emeralds?
Why are they carrying their official staffs
inlaid with silver and gold?

    Because the barbarians are coming today,
    and such things are known to dazzle barbarians.

Why don't the famous orators arrive as they always do
to pontificate at length and expound on their views?

Because the barbarians are coming today,
and they are bored by eloquence and long discourse.

Why has this anxiety come upon us all at once,
why such confusion? (How serious all the faces!)
Why are the streets and squares emptying so quickly,
and all the people returning to their homes so subdued?

Because night came and the barbarians never appeared.
Later some of our men arrived from the borders
and gave us the news: there were no more barbarians.

What are we going to do now, without barbarians?
Those people, they were a kind of solution.

Lies

Then, though there are many things we praise in Homer,
this we will not ... nor shall we approve of Aeschylus when
his Thetis avers that Apollo, singing at her wedding, fore-
told the happy fortunes of her issue:

> Their days prolonged, from pain and sickness free,
> and rounding out the tale of heaven's blessings,
> raised the proud paean, making glad my heart.
> And I believed that Phoebus' mouth divine,
> Filled with the breath of prophecy, could not lie,
> But he himself, the singer ...
> Is now the slayer of my son.
>
> Plato, *Republic* II

At the wedding of Peleus and Thetis
Apollo rose from the splendid table
to give his blessing to the newlyweds
and the offspring to come from their union.
He proclaimed: 'No illness shall touch him
and his life shall be long.' When he said this
Thetis took great joy, for the words of Apollo,
who was well versed in prophecy,
seemed a guarantee for her child.
And when Achilles grew tall and his beauty
became the talk of Thessaly,
Thetis recalled the words of the god.
But one day the elders came with news
that Achilles had been slain in Troy.
Thetis tore her purple robes;
she pulled off her bracelets and jewels
and hurled them to the ground.
In her grief she recalled that prophetic day
and asked what wise Apollo was up to:
where was the poet who spoke
so skilfully at table, where was the prophet

when they killed her son in the prime of his youth?
And the elders responded that it was Apollo
who had come down to Troy himself,
and with the Trojans had killed Achilles.

The Funeral of Sarpedon

Zeus is heavy with grief. Sarpedon
is dead at Patroclus' hands and, right now,
the son of Menoetius and his Achaeans are setting out
to steal the corpse and desecrate it.

But Zeus will not allow it.
He had left his beloved child alone
and now he's lost – for such the Law demanded.
But at least he will honour him in death.
Behold: he sends Phoebus down to the field
with orders to care for the body.

Phoebus lifts the hero's corpse with reverence
and pity, and bears him to the river.
He washes away the blood and dust
and closes the wounds, careful
not to leave a scar; he pours balm
of ambrosia over the body and clothes him
in resplendent Olympian robes.
He blanches the skin and with a comb of pearl
straightens the raven-black hair.
He lays him out, arranging the lovely limbs.

The youth seems a king, a charioteer,
twenty-five or twenty-six years old –
relishing his moment of victory,
with the swiftest stallions, upon a golden chariot
in a grand competition.

Phoebus, completing his assignment,
calls on his two siblings,
Sleep and Death, commanding them
to carry the body to Lycia, land of riches.

So the two brothers, Sleep and Death,
set out on foot to transport the body
to Lycia, land of riches.
And at the door of the king's palace
they hand over the glorious body
and return to their affairs.

As they receive him into the palace
they begin laments and tributes, processions
and libations flowing from sacred vessels
and everything that befits such a sad funeral;
then skilled craftsmen from the city
and artists well known for their work in marble
arrive to fashion the tomb and the stele.

The Horses of Achilles

When they saw Patroclus lying dead
who was once so brave, so strong and young,
the horses of Achilles began to weep;
their immortal nature stood aghast
at that masterwork of death.
They reared their heads and shook their manes,
they stamped the ground with their hooves
and mourned for Patroclus,
lifeless, destroyed, mere flesh and bone,
defenceless now, his spirit gone,
a castaway from life, now naught.

Zeus saw the tears of the immortal steeds
and grieved, saying, 'It was my mistake,
it was my thoughtlessness at Peleus' wedding.
We should never have given you as a gift, poor horses!
What business did you have among wretched
humankind, plaything of destiny, you whom neither death
nor the sorrows of old age torment. Men have tangled you
in their own miseries.' Yet the two noble horses
continued to pour out their tears
for the eternal misfortune of death.

PART II

POEMS 1905–1915

The City

You said: 'I will go to another land; I will try another sea.
Another city will turn up, better than this one.
Here everything I do is condemned in advance
and my heart – like a dead man's – lies buried.
How long can my mind remain in this swamp?
Wherever I turn, wherever I look, I gaze
on the ruins of my life here, where I've spent
and botched and wasted so many years.'

You will find no new land; you will find no other seas.
This city will follow you. You will wander the same
streets and grow old in the same neighbourhoods;
your hair will turn white in the same houses.
And you will always arrive in this city. Abandon any hope
of finding another place. No ship, no road can take you there.
For just as you've ruined your life here
in this backwater, you've destroyed it everywhere on earth.

The Satrapy

What a pity! Though you were destined
for great and worthy achievements,
this adverse fate of yours, on every occasion,
denies you both encouragement and success.
The same base habits always block your path,
along with the old pettiness and indifference.
And how horrible, that day when you finally give in
(the day you let yourself give in),
when you take flight on the road to Susa
and travel to the great King Artaxerxes,
who receives you favourably in his court,
offering you satrapies and all the rest.
And you, in desperation you accept them,
those objects for which you have no desire.
Your soul yearns for other things, it cries out
for the praise of the crowd and the Sophists;
the hard-won, priceless acclaim;
the Assembly, the Theatre, the Crown of Laurel.
How can Artaxerxes give you these?
Where will you find such things in your satrapy?
And without them, what kind of life will you have?

The Wise Perceive Imminent Events

The gods perceive future events, mortals present ones, and
the wise perceive those that are imminent.

> Philostratus, *Life of Apollonius of Tyana* VIII.7

Men have knowledge of the present.
As for the future, the gods know it,
alone and fully enlightened.
But for matters on the verge of occurring, things that
    are imminent,
these the wise perceive. Sometimes,

when they are deep in study, their hearing
is convulsed. The veiled hum of imminent events
approaches. And they listen rapt. Meanwhile,
out on the street, the people hear nothing.

The Ides of March

Beware of greatness, my soul.
And if you cannot master your ambitions entirely,
pursue them at least with circumspection and care.
The further you advance,
the more reason to be prudent and attentive.

And when you reach your goal, Caesar at last,
when you take on the attributes of such an illustrious man,
be especially cautious when you walk the street,
a ruler, conspicuous with your entourage.
And if some Artemidorus should emerge from the crowd
to approach you, holding a letter
and whispering hurriedly, 'Read this now.
It speaks of grave matters that bear directly upon you,'
do not fail to stop; do not fail to postpone
the pending interview or task; do not fail
to brush aside the passers-by who greet and salute you
(you'll see them later); even the Senate itself
can wait while you read, without delay,
the urgent message of Artemidorus.

Done

Amid fear and suspicion,
with startled minds and frightened eyes,
we pine and scheme over what steps to take
to avoid the certain
danger that threatens us so horribly.
Yet we are wrong. This was not the danger in store;
the portents were false
(or we never heard them, or failed to construe them properly).
It's some other disaster, precipitous, violent,
one we hadn't imagined,
that suddenly takes us unawares, and –
there's no time now – overcomes us.

The God Abandoning Antony

Suddenly, around midnight, when you hear
an invisible troupe of players pass
with exquisite music and solemn voices –
do not lament in vain your waning luck, the many deeds
undone, all of your life plans
gone astray; no, do not lament.
Emboldened now, and as one long prepared,
make your farewell to her, the Alexandria that is leaving.
Above all, do not fool yourself, do not say
it was just a dream, or that your ears deceived you;
do not stoop to such empty hopes.
Emboldened now, and as one long prepared,
as is fitting for someone like you, worthy of such a city,
approach the window steadily
and listen, stirred, but not to the point
of whining or complaining as cowards do.
Let that music be your final joy,
the exquisite instruments of that mysterious troupe,
and make your farewell to her, the Alexandria you are losing.

Theodotus

If you are one of the truly elect
take care how you achieve your eminence.
For however roundly you are acclaimed,
however stridently the client-states may glorify
your exploits in Italy and Thessaly,
however many honorific decrees
your acolytes may publish in Rome,
neither your joy nor your triumph will long endure;
nor will you see yourself as some higher being – higher
    indeed! –
when, in Alexandria, Theodotus brings you,
on a bloodied plate,
the head of wretched Pompey.

And take no comfort in the presumption
that your own life, circumscribed, regular, prosaic,
will not admit such shocking, frightful events.
Perhaps, at this very moment,
at your neighbour's tidy house,
Theodotus is entering – invisible, incorporeal –
bearing such a horrific head.

Monotony

One monotonous day follows another
monotonous day, without change. The same
things happen, then happen again.
The same moments approach, then grow distant.

A month passes and brings another month.
Anyone can guess what's coming after:
all the tedious events from the day before,
until tomorrow looks nothing like tomorrow.

Ithaca

When you start on your way to Ithaca,
pray that the journey be long,
rich in adventure, rich in discovery.
Do not fear the Cyclops, the Laestrygonians
or the anger of Poseidon. You'll not encounter them
on your way if your thoughts remain high,
if a rare emotion possesses you body and soul.
You will not encounter the Cyclops,
the Laestrygonians or savage Poseidon
if you do not carry them in your own soul,
if your soul does not set them before you.

Pray that the journey be a long one,
that there be countless summer mornings
when, with what pleasure, what joy,
you drift into harbours never before seen;
that you make port in Phoenician markets
and purchase their lovely goods:
coral and mother of pearl, ebony and amber,
and every kind of delightful perfume.
Acquire all the voluptuous perfumes that you can,
then sail to Egypt's many towns
to learn and learn from their scholars.

Always keep Ithaca fixed in your mind.
Arrival there is your destination.
Yet do not hurry the journey at all:
better that it lasts for many years
and you arrive an old man on the island,
rich from all that you have gained on the way,
not counting on Ithaca for riches.

For Ithaca gave you the splendid voyage:
without her you would never have embarked.
She has nothing more to give you now.

And though you find her poor, she has not misled you;
you having grown so wise, so experienced from your travels,
by then you will have learned what Ithacas mean.

As Much As You Can

If you cannot fashion your life as you would like,
endeavour to do this at least,
as much as you can: do not trivialize it
through too much contact with the world,
through too much activity and chatter.

Do not trivialize your life by parading it,
running around displaying it
in the daily stupidity
of cliques and gatherings
until it becomes like a tiresome guest.

Trojans

Our labours are those of men trapped in failure;
our labours are like those of the Trojans.
We make some slight progress, take on
a bit more, begin to grow bold
and have high hopes.

But something always intervenes and stops us:
Achilles emerges from the trench before us
and with his war-cry frightens us away.

Our labours are like those of the Trojans:
we imagine that with resolution and courage
we can reverse the decline in our fortunes,
and so we stand outside the walls, girded for battle.

But when the terrible moment arrives,
all our resolution and courage vanish;
our spirit is shaken, paralysed in fear,
and we run round and round the walls
trying to save ourselves by flight.

Yet our demise is certain. High up
on the walls, the lament has already begun.
Our feelings and the memories of our days all weep.
Priam and Hecuba weep for us bitterly.

King Demetrius

> As if he were not a king, but a player,
> he disguised himself with a grey mantle
> in exchange for his tragic one,
> and, escaping notice, departed.
> Plutarch, *Life of Demetrius* XLIV

When the Macedonians abandoned him,
showing their preference for Pyrrhus,
King Demetrius (that great-souled man)
did not comport himself – so they say –
like a king in the least. He went
and unfastened his golden robes,
threw off his purple buskins,
hurriedly dressed in simple clothes
and left, behaving just like an actor who,
when the curtain falls,
changes his costume and departs.

The Glory of the Ptolemies

I am King Lagides, absolute master
(through my power and wealth) of sensual pleasure.
There is no one, Macedonian or barbarian,
who is my match, or even comes near.
That seeming Seleucid is a buffoon, a vulgar voluptuary.
But if it is something else you are seeking, take this to heart:
this city is the teacher, the crown of all Hellas,
wisest in every subject, and every art.

The Procession of Dionysus

The sculptor Damon (who has no peer throughout
the Peloponnese) is fashioning in Parian marble
a 'Procession of Dionysus'. Behold the god
in front, in celestial glory, with steady stride.
Behind him is Licence, at whose side
Intoxication stands, pouring wine for satyrs
from an amphora twined with ivy. Effete
Sweetwine sits nearby, eyes closing, sleep
inducing. Further back trail the singers,
Melody and Tunesweet; after them, Revelry,
keeping the procession's solemn torch aflame;
then modest Ceremony. All these figures
Damon carves. Meanwhile in his mind he adds up
the payment due him from the Syracusan king:
three talents, a huge amount. With this income,
when it arrives, along with his other holdings,
he can live high, a man of means; he can even
go into politics – what joy! – and he too, one day,
will have his say in the assembly and in the forum.

The Battle of Magnesia

He has lost his former valour, his courage.
Now it is this tired body, his infirm carriage

that will be his chief concern. The rest
of his life will run its course in quiet. At least,

so Philip says. Tonight he's playing dice;
is of a mind to amuse himself. Set roses

on the banqueting table! So what if Antiochus today
has been utterly routed in Magnesia. They say

his splendid army was completely decimated.
It can't be true. Surely the loss was overstated?

Or so one hopes: though foes in battle, we were one race.
But a single 'one hopes' will suffice. Perhaps more than
    suffice.

Philip certainly will not postpone the feast.
However hard his life may have been, at least

one good remains: his full memory he has kept:
and he well recalls just how much the Syrians wept

when Macedonia, their mother, was scorched.
Let the dinner begin. Slaves! Flutes! Torches!

The Displeasure of the Seleucid

The Seleucid Demetrius was far from pleased
when he learned that a Ptolemy had arrived
in Italy and in such a pitiful state,
with only three or four servants to escort him,
dressed in rags and journeying on foot. At this rate
they'd end up a joke, the royal family the laughing stock
of Rome. That they've become, in point of fact,
a kind of servant to the Romans,
this the Seleucid knows; that the Romans
arbitrarily dispense or withhold their thrones
as pleasure dictates, this too he knows. But at least
in their appearance they might retain some dignity
and not forget that they are still kings,
that they still (alas!) bear the title of king.

Hence the displeasure of the Seleucid, Demetrius;
and straight away he offered Ptolemy
robes of purple, a shining crown,
costly diamonds, a host of attendants, and a retinue
that included his most expensive stallions,
to announce his presence in Rome as befits
an Alexandrian king, a Greek monarch.

But Lagides, who had come to solicit,
knew his business and refused the gifts;
he had no need for such luxuries.
He entered Rome modestly, in shabby old clothes,
and lodged at the home of a craftsman.
Later he presented himself as a poor fellow,
a pauper before the Senate,
to have better success in his begging.

Orophernes

The figure depicted on this tetradrachmon
with what appears to be a smile on his face,
that beautiful, delicate face,
is Orophernes, son of Ariarathus.

As a child they exiled him from Cappadocia,
led him out of his fathers' grand palace
and sent him to Ionia, to come of age there
and be forgotten, surrounded by strangers.

Ah, those elegant Ionian nights where,
without fear and in a manner thoroughly Hellenic,
he came to know pleasure in all its fullness.
In his heart he was always the Asiatic,
but in his comportment and speech he was Greek,
decked out with turquoise stones, wearing Greek dress,
his body perfumed in jasmine balm.
Of all the beautiful youths in Ionia
he was the most handsome, the ideal.

Later, when the Syrians entered Cappadocia
and made him king,
he threw himself into the role of monarch
in order to delight himself each day in some novel manner,
to amass a hoard of gold and silver
and to smile and exult
at the sight of such treasures, heaped and gleaming.
As for any concern for the state or its administration –
he was blind to all that was happening around him.

The Cappadocians quickly ousted him,
and he ended up in Syria, in the palace
of Demetrius, where he lazed about and amused himself.

One day, however, unaccustomed reflections
breached his habitual indolence. He remembered
that on his mother Antiochis' side
and through his aged grandmother Stratonice
he too had a claim to Syria's throne,
he too, in fact, was almost a Seleucid.
He briefly shook himself free from his lust
and drunkenness and, dizzied and incompetent,
tried to begin an intrigue,
to take some action, to form a plan,
but he failed pitifully and was set at naught.

His death, somewhere, will have been recorded and lost;
or perhaps history has passed over it entirely.
Perhaps history itself, and with good reason, would not
condescend to recall so slight a matter.

The figure depicted on this tetradrachmon
shows the grace of his lovely youth,
the remaining trace of his poetic beauty,
a voluptuous memento of that Ionian boy,
Orophernes, son of Ariarathus.

Alexandrian Kings

The people of Alexandria had all gathered
to see the children of Cleopatra,
Caesarion and his younger brothers,
Alexander and Ptolemy, who for the first time
were being displayed in the Gymnasium,
to be proclaimed kings there
amid the shining spectacle of a military parade.

They proclaimed Alexander king of Armenia,
of Media and of the Parthians.
They proclaimed Ptolemy king
of Cilicia, Syria and Phoenicia.
Caesarion stood out in front,
dressed in silk the colour of roses,
on his breast a bouquet of hyacinths,
his belt a double stitch of sapphires and amethysts,
his sandals bound with white ribbons
and embroidered with rose-coloured pearls.
Caesarion they proclaimed even higher than his younger
        brothers:
They proclaimed him King of Kings.

The Alexandrians understood, of course,
that this was mere words and theatre.

But the day was warm and poetic,
the sky an expanse of blue,
and the Gymnasium of Alexandria
a veritable triumph of art.
The luxury of the courtiers was exquisite;
Caesarion himself, grace and beauty incarnate
(the son of Cleopatra, the blood of the Lagids),
and the Alexandrians flocked to the feast,

showing their support and offering cheers
in Greek, Egyptian and some in Hebrew,
thoroughly enchanted by the lovely spectacle –
knowing all the time what these things really meant;
what empty words all these kingships were.

Philhellene

Take care that the engraving is done skilfully;
the expression sober and dignified. Better, perhaps,
to make the crown a bit narrower at the top;
I don't like the wide ones favoured by the Parthians.
The inscription, as usual, should be in Greek;
nothing exaggerated, nothing pompous –
we don't want the proconsul to misconstrue it;
he's always sniffing about for something to complain to
      Rome –
but still, of course, it must be properly honorific.
We'll want something very special for the obverse,
perhaps a discus-thrower, young, handsome.
But, above all, I urge you to make absolutely certain
(for god's sake, Sithaspes, don't let them overlook it),
after 'King' and 'Saviour' make sure
they inscribe in elegant lettering 'Philhellene'.
And don't start now with your cavilling,
saying, 'What Greeks?' and 'What's so Greek
about this place, here behind Zagros, beyond Phraata?'
There are many people far more barbaric than ourselves,
and since they describe themselves as Greek, we'll write it too.
And besides, don't forget that, on occasion,
Syrian sophists do, in fact, come to our city,
as well as rhymesters and other useless pedants.
So we are not, I think, altogether bereft of the Hellenic.

The Footsteps

On an ebony bedstead
adorned with eagles made of coral,
Nero lies deep in sleep – quiet, unconscious, happy:
in the prime of his body's vigour;
in the beautiful ardour of his youth.

But in the alabaster hall
that holds the ancient shrine of the Ahenobarbi,
the Lares of his house are anxious.
These minor household gods are trembling,
trying to conceal their already negligible bodies.
For they heard a terrible noise,
a deadly sound spiralling up the staircase,
iron-soled footsteps shaking the steps.
The miserable Lares, near-fainting now,
huddle in the corner of the shrine,
jostling and stumbling over each other,
one little god falling over the next,
for they knew what sort of noise it was;
they recognize, by now, the footsteps of the Furies.

Herodes Atticus

Herodes Atticus – there's glory for you!

Alexander of Seleucia, one of our top sophists,
arriving in Athens to teach,
finds the city deserted. And why?
Herodes was at his country house. All the youth
had followed him there to hear his lectures.
In view of this, Alexander the sophist
writes to Herodes and requests
that he send the Greeks back to Athens.
Tactful Herodes responds straight away:
'I am coming, and with me, the Greeks.'

How many young men now in Alexandria,
Antioch or Beirut
(our future orators, trained in Hellenism),
gathering at the most sought-after tables –
where they sometimes discuss literature
and sometimes their own delicious affairs –
suddenly gaze in silent abstraction.
They leave their glasses untouched
and muse on the good fortune of Herodes –
for what other sophist can claim such distinction? –
that the Greeks (the Greeks!) should follow him
in all he wishes and in all he does,
abandoning judgement, abandoning debate,
abandoning even choice, simply to follow him.

Tyanian Sculptor

As you may have heard, I am not without experience
in the field. A good deal of stone
has passed under these hands. Back in my home town, in
       Tyana,
I am quite well known; and here too senators
have commissioned many pieces from my workshop.

Allow me to show you several
right now. Over here there is a Rhea,
solemn, redolent of fortitude, done in a strictly archaic style.
Here we have a Pompey, a Marius,
an Aemilius Paullus and a Scipio Africanus. Each likeness
rendered as faithfully as my talents allowed.
Observe here a Patroclus (I will retouch it soon)
and in that corner where you see those fragments
of yellow marble, that is Caesarion.

I have been busy for some time now
working on a Poseidon. His horses present, I think,
the greatest formal challenge; that is, how to fashion
the animals in such a way that they appear light, even
       weightless,
so that their bodies and their hooves make perfectly clear
that they are not treading on the earth, but cantering over
       the water.

But here is the work that is most dear to me,
the one over which I've laboured with the greatest care and
       devotion;
one day, in the heat of summer,
when my mind was sojourning amid the ideal forms,
it was this figure I dreamed of, this young Hermes.

The Tomb of the Grammarian Lysias

Just on the right as you enter the library of Beirut,
that is where we buried the learned grammarian,
Lysias. The place we chose suits him perfectly.
For we interred him next to those things he recalls
perhaps even now – scholia, texts, grammars,
variant readings, volumes of idiomatic dictionaries.
And we too, in this way, will be able to acknowledge
and honour his grave, when we pass among these books.

The Tomb of Eurion

In this exquisitely fashioned monument
made entirely of syenite and covered
with numberless lilies and violets
lies handsome Eurion,
a youth from Alexandria, twenty-five years old.
Of ancient Macedonian stock on his father's side;
from a long line of Jewish magistrates on his mother's.
He studied philosophy with Aristocleitus
and rhetoric with Paros. In Thebes he learned
to construe the sacred texts. He composed a local history
of the prefecture of Arsinoe. That one work, at least,
will survive. But the most precious of his gifts – his body –
we have lost: it was like a vision of Apollo.

That's the Man!

A stranger – unknown in Antioch – originally
from Edessa and always scribbling. Behold, finally,
the last ode is done. Counting this one

he will have eighty-three poems in total. But all that writing,
the focus on versification, the concentration
required to get the right balance of phrase in the Greek:
it has utterly exhausted the poet. Now the slightest thing
weighs him down.

But one thought lifts him suddenly out of his lethargy –
the delicious 'That's the man!'
that Lucian once heard in his sleep.

Dangerous Things

Myrtias, a Syrian studying in Alexandria
during the reigns of Constans and Constantius,
half pagan and half Christian convert:
'Fortified with contemplation and long study,
I will not fear my passions, like a coward;
I will give my body entirely to pleasure,
to dreamed-of joys, the most brazen
erotic desires, the most depraved passions in my blood,
all without fear. For when I so wish it –
and I *will* so wish it, fortified as I'll be
with contemplation and long study –
at those critical moments I will find again
my ascetic spirit, as pure as it was before.'

Manuel Comnenus

One melancholy September day
the emperor, Lord Manuel Comnenus,
sensed that his end was near. The astrologers
of the court (men in his pay) droned on
how he would live for many years still.
But while they go on with their talk,
he recalls forgotten habits of piety
and from the monastic cells he orders
ecclesiastical vestments be brought;
he puts them on and delights to appear
in the modest guise of a priest or monk.

Happy are those who believe
and who end their days, like the emperor Lord Manuel,
humbly clad in their faith.

In Church

I love the church – its winged seraphim,
its silver vessels and candlesticks,
the lights, the icons and the pulpit.

When I enter a Greek church
with its incense floating in the air,
the liturgical voices and harmonies,
the majesty of the attending priests,
the solemn rhythm of their movements –
all resplendent in their ornate vestments –
my thoughts turn to the glory of our race:
the grandeur of our Byzantine past.

Very Seldom

An old man, stooped and spent,
crippled by the years and by excess,
walks slowly across the alley.
But as he enters his house
to hide his wretched state and his old age,
he muses on that share of youth he still claims.

Young boys today recite his verses.
His fancies pass across their waking eyes.
Their healthy, sensuous minds,
their muscular, smooth limbs,
are stirred by his vision of beauty.

Of the Shop

He wraps them up carefully, neatly
in fine green silk of the highest quality:

roses made of rubies, lilies made of pearls,
violets of amethyst. Whatever he wills

he creates and judges it beautiful – but not
as he ever saw or studied them in nature. He puts

them in the cabinet, examples of his daring and skill
at craftsmanship. When a customer comes in he will

display some other items – still first-rate things –
bracelets and chains, necklaces and rings.

Painted Things

I love my work and take pains with it. But today
I find the slow pace of composition discouraging.
The weather has got into me. It just gets darker
and darker. Non-stop wind and rain.
I'd rather watch than write.
I'm looking at this painting now:
it shows a handsome boy lying near a spring,
out of breath from running.
Such a beautiful boy! And such a divine noon
which has taken him and induced him to sleep!
I sit and gaze like this for a long time.
Immersed again in art, I recover from the labour of
     creating it.

Morning Sea

Let me stop right here. Let me, too, have a look at nature:
the morning sea and the cloudless sky,
both a luminous blue, the yellow shore, all of it
beautiful, and in such magnificent light.

Let me stop right here. Let me pretend this is actually
what I'm seeing (I really did see it, when I first stopped)
and not, here too, more of those fantasies of mine,
more of those memories, those voluptuous illusions.

Ionic

Although we've broken their statues,
although we've driven them from their temples,
the gods have not perished from this, not at all.
Land of Ionia, it is you they love still,
it is you their souls remember.
When an August morning dawns above you,
the air trembles with ardour from their life;
and sometimes an ethereal, adolescent form,
indistinct, in rapid flight,
wings his way across your hills.

The Café Entrance

Something they said beside me
turned my attention towards the café entrance.
There I saw a beautiful body
that Eros must have fashioned with his boundless skill,
designing with delight the symmetrical limbs,
moulding the tall, sculpted frame,
tenderly drawing the face,
and bestowing, with a touch of his hand,
a feeling on the brow, in the eyes and on the lips.

One Night

The room was shabby and miserable,
tucked above a suspect tavern.
A window opened on to the alley,
narrow and unclean. From the tavern beneath
came the voices of workmen
playing cards and carousing.

There, in that humble, commonplace bed,
I possessed the body of love; I possessed
those sensual, rose-red lips of intoxication –
red lips so intoxicating that even now,
as I write these lines, after so many years
all alone in this house, I am drunk with it again.

Return

Return often and take me,
beloved sensation, return and take me –
when the body's memory awakens,
and old longings pulse again in my blood,
when lips and skin remember,
and hands could almost touch again.

Return often and take me at night,
when lips and skin remember.

Far Away

I would like to speak of this memory . . .
But it has grown dim . . . as if no trace of it remains –
for it lies far off in the first years of my youth.

Skin as if made of jasmine . . .
an August evening – was it August? –
I barely recall the eyes now: they were blue, I think.
Ah yes . . . blue, a sapphire blue.

He Vows

Every now and then   he vows to live a better life.
But when night comes   with her own counsels,
with her promises   and her compromises,
when night comes   with her power
over the body   that seeks and yearns,
he returns, lost,   to the same fatal pleasures.

I Left

I allowed no restraint. I gave in completely and left.
I ran toward pleasures that were half real
and half spun by my own mind.
I ran in the radiant night
and drank down strong wines, the kind
that champions of pleasure drink.

Chandelier

In a small, empty room, nothing
but four walls covered in green fabric,
an elegant chandelier glows, ablaze with light;
and in each of the chandelier's flames
burns an erotic fever, an erotic urge.

The fire raging in the chandelier
fills the tiny room, which shines
with a radiance that is in no way familiar.
And from its heat comes a kind of pleasure
not suited for timid bodies.

PART III

POEMS 1916–1918

Since Nine O'Clock

Half past twelve. The time has passed quickly
since I first lit the lamp at nine o'clock,
and sat down here. I've sat without reading,
without speaking. With whom could I speak,
all alone in this house?

Since nine o'clock when I lit the lamp
a ghostly image of my adolescent body
came to me, reminding me
of closed and scented chambers,
and past pleasures – what brazen pleasures!
It brought before my eyes
streets now unrecognizable,
bars once filled with movement, now closed,
cafés and theatres that once existed.

The vision of my body in its youth
brought sorrowful memories also:
the grieving of my family, separations,
the feelings I had for my own kin, feelings
for the dead, whom I little acknowledged.

Half past twelve; how the time has passed.
Half past twelve; how the years have passed.

Insight

The years of my youth, my sensual adolescence –
how clearly I see their meaning now.

All those excessive, useless regrets . . .

I didn't see the meaning then.

For in the dissolute life of my youth
the plans for my poetry were taking shape;
the boundaries of my art were being drawn.

That's why my regrets were never firm,
and my determination to refrain, to change my ways,
lasted two weeks at most.

Before the Statue of Endymion

Upon a white chariot drawn by four mules
of purest white, silver-strapped with jewels,
I came from Miletus to Latmus.
I sailed from Alexandria in a trireme of Tyrian purple
to discharge the sacred rites of Endymion – sacrifices
and libations. Behold, the statue. In ecstasy now
I contemplate the famous beauty of Endymion.
My servants empty baskets of jasmine, and auspicious
prayers arouse the pleasure of ancient times.

Envoys from Alexandria

It had been centuries since they'd seen gifts in Delphi
as grand as those sent by the two brothers,
the rival Ptolemaic kings. But once they'd received the gifts,
the priests grew nervous about the oracle.
They would need all of their great skill, all their tact,
to determine the appropriate response; that is,
which of the two, which of *those* two, will be thwarted in his
    wish.
They convene at night and in secret
to debate the claims and counterclaims of the Lagid family.

But look, the envoys are back. They offer their salutations.
They are returning, so they say, to Alexandria,
and make no mention of the oracle. The priests rejoice at the
    news
(the splendid gifts, it's understood, are theirs to keep)
but they seem baffled, unable to interpret this sudden
    indifference.
They do not know that yesterday the envoys received the
    news:
the oracle was given at Rome; it was there that the kingdom
    was divided.

Aristobulus

The palace laments, the king grieves,
King Herod sobs inconsolably.
The whole country is mourning for Aristobulus,
who drowned tragically
playing in the water with his friends.

When they learn of his death in distant lands,
when the news is carried to Syria,
even the Greeks will join in mourning;
all the poets and sculptors will lament
when word of Aristobulus has spread.
For what other imagined ephebe had roused
their fancy as had the beauty of this youth;
and what statue of a god could Antioch boast
that matched the beauty of this son of Israel?

His mother, the First Princess, keens
and laments; first among the Hebrew women,
Queen Alexandra mourns her loss.
But when she is alone her sorrow changes
to groans and raging, rants and curses.
How they tricked her! How they pulled the wool over her
    eyes!
They finally achieved their end.
They've brought the house of the Hasmoneans to ruin.
How did he do it, the villain king?
The scheming, vicious, depraved king.
How did he do it? It was a plot so fiendish
that even Miriam knew nothing about it.
If only Miriam had had some hint, if she'd suspected
    anything,
she'd have found a way to save her brother;
she's a queen after all; she could have done something.
How they'll rejoice now, laughing in secret,
those vicious women, Cyprus and Salome;

those debased creatures, Cyprus and Salome.
And to be powerless, to be compelled
to pretend she believes their lies,
unable to speak freely to her people,
to go and cry out to the Hebrews,
to tell them, to explain how this murder was done.

Caesarion

In part to verify a date,
and in part just to pass the time,
last night I picked up a volume
of Ptolemaic inscriptions and began reading.
Those endless poems of praise and flattery
all sound the same. All the men are brilliant,
great and good, mighty benefactors;
most wise in all their undertakings.
The same for the women of the dynasty, all the Berenices
and Cleopatras, wonderful, each and every one.

When I managed to find the date in question,
I'd have put the book aside had a brief mention
of King Caesarion, an insignificant note really,
not suddenly caught my eye . . .

Ah, there you stood, with that vague
charm of yours. And since history has devoted
just a few lines to you, I had more freedom
to fashion you in my mind's eye . . .
I made you handsome, capable of deep feeling.
My art gave your face an appealing,
dreamlike beauty. In fact, I imagined you
so vividly last night, that when my lamp
went out – I let it go out on purpose –
I actually thought you had come into my room;
you were there, standing before me,
just as you would have looked in defeated Alexandria,
pale and tired, ideal in your sorrow,
still hoping for mercy from those vicious men
who kept on whispering 'too many Caesars'.

Nero's Deadline

Nero was not particularly concerned when he heard
the Delphic oracle's prophecy:
'Years seventy and three beware.'
He still had plenty of time to enjoy himself.
He is only thirty. The deadline appointed
by the god seems far enough away
to take precautions about any future dangers.

He will return to Rome now a bit fatigued,
but fatigued in a delicious way from this journey
where every day provided some new delight –
in the Greek theatres, the gardens and gymnasia ...
the evenings spent in the towns of Achaea ...
and yes, above all, the joy of those naked bodies ...

So much for Nero. Meanwhile, in Spain, Galba
secretly recruits and trains his forces,
an old man, aged seventy-three.

In the Seaport

Young Emes, twenty-eight years of age,
sailed in a Tenian ship to this Syrian seaport,
hoping to learn the perfume trade. But he fell sick
on the way and as soon as he put ashore
he died. His pauper's burial took place here.
A few hours before he passed away
he whispered something about 'home' and 'parents,
very old'. But who they were no one had a clue,
nor where in all of Greece he called home.
So much the better. For now,
although he lies here dead in this eastern seaport,
his parents will go on thinking he's alive.

One of Their Gods

When one of them passed through the forum
of Seleucia just as night began to fall,
young, tall, perfect in his beauty,
with the joy of imperishability in his eyes
and his aromatic black hair,
the passers-by would stare,
asking each other if they knew the man:
was he a Greek from Syria, or a foreigner?
But some, who watched with greater attention,
understood and drew aside for him to pass;
and as he vanished under the arcades,
amid the shadow and light of evening,
proceeding to that neighbourhood
which comes alive only at night, with orgies and
     debauchery,
every kind of drunkenness and lust,
they wondered which of Them he might be,
and for which of his suspect passions
had he come down to the streets of Seleucia
from the Venerable and Sacred Abodes.

The Tomb of Lanes

Marcus, the Lanes whom you loved is not here
in this tomb where you visit and weep for hours.
The Lanes whom you loved is nearer, Marcus,
when you close yourself in your room and gaze on his
    portrait;
that image preserved all that was worthy in him;
that image preserved all that you loved.

Do you remember, Marcus, when you brought
from the proconsul's palace the famous painter from Cyrene,
and as soon as he laid eyes on your friend,
he tried to persuade you with his artist's cunning
that he should draw him, without question, as Hyacinth
(that way the portrait would garner more fame)?

But your Lanes didn't put his beauty on loan like that;
firmly opposing the man, he demanded to be portrayed
not as Hyacinth, nor as anyone else,
but as Lanes, son of Rhametichus, an Alexandrian.

The Tomb of Iases

Here I lie, Iases, of this great city
the youth most renowned in beauty.
Distinguished scholars admired me,
as did undistinguishing, simple folk. I rejoiced equally

in both. But being the world's Narcissus or Hermes,
all the excess sapped and destroyed me. Passer-by,
if you are Alexandrian, you will not judge too severely; you
    see
how passionate our life is; what warmth it has; what supreme
    pleasure.

In a Town of Osroene

Around midnight yesterday they carried our friend Remon
back to our house after he was wounded in a tavern brawl.
The moon cast its light through the window, open all night,
and fell across his beautiful body, there on the bed.
We're a mixed lot here: Syrians, Greeks, Armenians, Medes.
Such is Remon too. But yesterday, when the moon
traced its light across that sensuous face of his,
it was Plato's *Charmides* that came to mind.

The Tomb of Ignatius

I am no longer that Cleon, once so famous
in Alexandria (where they are not easily impressed)
for my splendid houses, my gardens,
my horses and carriages,
for the jewellery and silks I used to wear.
All that is foreign to me now. I am not that Cleon here.
Let those twenty-eight years be erased.
Here I am Ignatius, reciter of the liturgy, who far too late
came to his senses; and thus have I lived ten happy months
in the serenity and safety of Christ.

In the Month of Athyr

I can hardly make out on the ancient stone:
'Lo[rd] Jesus Christ'. A 'so[u]l' I discern
and 'In the mon[th] of Athyr ... Leukio[s] came to [re]st'.
There's mention of his age: 'He li[ve]d to be –'
The 'Kappa-Zeta' means he came to rest quite young.
In the corroded part: 'Hi[m] ... Alexandrian'.
The next three lines are badly effaced,
but several words stand out – 'our t[ea]rs' and 'pain',
then once more 'tears' and 'a sorrow to h[i]s [f]riends'.
In love, it seems, Leukios was blessed.
In the month of Athyr, Leukios came to rest.

For Ammones, Who Died at
Twenty-nine, in the Year 610

Raphael, they are asking that you write
several verses for the epitaph of the poet Ammones.
Something refined and tasteful. You can do it.
You're the right man to compose a fitting tribute
for the poet Ammones, one of our very own.

Of course you will devote a few words to his verses –
but you must also speak about his beauty,
his delicate beauty that we loved so much.

Your Greek is always so fine and musical,
but this will require all of your skill now.
For into a foreign tongue all our sorrow and love must flow.
Pour out all of your Egyptian feeling into that foreign
    tongue.

Raphael, these verses must be written, you understand,
so that they retain something of our own life in them,
so that every beat and every phrase give clear proof
that an Alexandrian is writing about an Alexandrian.

Aemilianus Monai, Alexandrian, AD *628-655*

'With words, gestures and my general demeanour
I will forge an excellent suit of armour;
and wearing it I will confront all who wish me ill
with no feeling of weakness or fear.

'They may wish to do me harm but, confused
by all the lies I've spread around me,
any who approach will be confounded
when they look for weak spots or wounds.'

Boastful words from Aemilianus Monai.
Did he ever forge such a suit of armour?
If he did, he didn't wear it long.
He died in Sicily, twenty-seven years old.

When They Come Alive

Try to preserve them, poet,
your visions of love,
however few may stay for you.
Cast them, half hidden, into your verse.
Try to hold on to them, poet,
when they come alive in your mind
at night or in the brightness of noon.

Pleasure

The joy and balm of my life is the memory of those hours
when I found and held pleasure just as I had wished it.
The joy and balm of my life is that I was able to avoid
any sensual gratification that seemed routine.

I Have Gazed So Much

I have gazed so much on beauty
that my eyes overflow with it.

The body's curves. Red lips. Voluptuous limbs.
Hair as if taken from a Greek statue,
always lovely, even if uncombed,
tumbling lightly over the snowy brow:
the Dramatis Personae of love that my poetry
demanded . . . in the nights of my youth,
encountered, secretly, in those nights . . .

In the Street

His face, appealing, a little wan;
his languid eyes a chestnut colour;
twenty-five years old but seeming twenty,
with an artist's sense for clothing –
the colour of the tie, the collar's shape –
aimlessly wandering the street
as if still dazed from the illicit passion,
the quite illicit passion he has just enjoyed.

The Tobacconist's Window

Near the brightly lit window
of a tobacconist's shop, they stood amid a crowd of people.
By chance their gazes met
and hesitantly they half expressed
the illicit longing of their flesh.
Later, after several anxious steps along the pavement –
they smiled and gently nodded.

Then the closed carriage . . .
the sensuous mingling of their bodies;
the hands, the lips coming together.

The Passage

Those things he only timidly imagined as a schoolboy
stand open now, revealed before him.
He goes to parties, stays out all night,
gets swept off his feet. And this is perfectly fitting (for our
　　art, that is)
as his blood, young and hot,
is pleasure's prize. Lawless, erotic ecstasy
overcomes his body. And his young limbs
give in. In this way a simple youth
becomes worthy of our regard, and briefly he too
crosses over to the Exalted World of Poetry –
this appealing boy with his blood young and hot.

In the Evening

It would not have lasted long in any case.
Years of experience taught me that. And yet,
it was rather hasty, the way Fate ended it.
The good times were brief.
But how powerful the fragrances;
how wonderful the bed we lay in;
what pleasure we gave our bodies!

An echo from those days of pleasure,
an echo from those days came near,
an ember from our youth's fire;
I took one of his letters
and read it over and over until the light faded.

Melancholic, I stepped out on to the balcony –
I stepped out to change my mood by seeing at least
a little of this city that I love,
a little movement in the streets and in the shops.

Grey

Gazing upon a half-grey opal
I suddenly recalled two beautiful grey eyes
I'd once seen. It must have been twenty years ago ...

We were lovers for a month.
Then he left; to Smyrna I think,
looking for work, and we never saw each other again.

Their beauty must have dimmed by now – if he's even alive –
    those grey eyes;
that beautiful face has surely gone to ruin.

Memory, keep those eyes just as they were.
And memory, whatever you can salvage of that passion of
    mine,
whatever you can, bring back to me tonight.

Beside the House

Yesterday, strolling in a remote neighbourhood,
I passed beside the house
I had entered when I was just a boy.
It was there that Eros first seized my limbs
with his delicious force.

And yesterday,
as I crossed that same old street, suddenly,
through the enchantment that Eros gives,
it was all made beautiful again ... the shops, the pavements,
    the stones,
the walls and terraces and windows;
nothing unseemly remained.

And while I stood there, gazing up at the door,
while I stood loitering beside the house,
my entire being exuded
a sensual feeling confined within.

The Next Table

He can't be more than twenty-two.
And yet I'm certain it was at least that many years ago
that I enjoyed the very same body.

This isn't some erotic fantasy.
I've only just come into the casino
and there hasn't been time enough to drink.
I tell you, that's the very same body I once enjoyed.

And if I can't recall precisely where – that means nothing.

Now that he's sitting there at the next table,
I recognize each of his movements – and beneath his clothes
I see those beloved, naked limbs again.

Remember, Body . . .

Body, remember not only how deeply you were loved,
not only the many beds where you lay,
but also those desires that flashed
openly in their eyes
or trembled in the voice – and were thwarted
by some chance impediment.
Now that all of them are locked away in the past,
it almost seems as if you surrendered
to even those pre-empted desires – how they flashed,
    remember,
in the eyes of those who looked at you, how they trembled
in the voice for you, remember, body.

Days of 1903

I never found them again – so quickly lost,
the poetic eyes, the pallid face,
seen on the street at nightfall.

I never found them again – possessed entirely by chance,
then given up so easily,
and now so agonizingly longed for.
The poetic eyes, the pallid face,
those lips I never found again.

PART IV

POEMS 1919–1933

The Afternoon Sun

This room, how well I know it.
Now they're renting it and the one next door
as commercial space. The whole house is now
offices for brokers, salesmen, entire firms.

Ah, this room, how familiar it is!

Here, near the door, stood the sofa,
a Turkish carpet just before it;
nearby was a shelf with two yellow vases;
on the right – no, facing it – was an armoire with a mirror.
The desk where he wrote stood in the middle,
along with three large, wicker chairs.
Beside the window lay the bed
where we made love so many times.

All of these poor old furnishings must still exist somewhere.

Beside the window lay the bed;
the afternoon sunlight reached only half way across it . . .

That afternoon, at four o'clock, we parted,
just for a week . . . alas,
that week became forever.

To Live

It must have been one o'clock in the morning,
or one-thirty.

In a corner of the tavern;
behind the wooden partition.
Except for us, the space entirely empty.
An oil lamp was barely glowing.
The waiter on the night shift lay dozing at the door.

No one could have seen us. Regardless,
we'd reached such a state already,
we were past all thought of caution.

Our clothes half undone now – the few we had on,
with divine July burning.

Gratification of the flesh
between half-opened clothes,
the quick baring of the flesh – the ideal image of it
has travelled across twenty-six years, and now has come
to live in these verses.

Of the Jews, AD 50

Painter and poet, sprinter and discus-thrower,
with Endymion's beauty, Ianthes, son of Antony,
of a family dear to the Synagogue:

'My proudest days are those
when I leave behind all sensuous pursuits,
when I abandon hard, beautiful Hellenism,
with its sovereign ideal
of perfectly formed and perishable white limbs,
and I become that which I hope
forever to remain: a son of the Jews, of the Holy Jews.'

Too fervent, his confession: 'Forever to remain
of the Jews, of the Holy Jews . . .'

He didn't remain that at all.
Pleasure and the fine arts of Alexandria
kept him their passionate disciple.

Imenos

'. . . To be cherished with even greater zeal
is that pleasure which is procured morbidly and through
     corruption.
Seldom is a body found able to endure what is required.
Morbidly, through corruption, one attains a level of sensual
     intensity
that health can never know.'

Passage from a letter
of the young Imenos (of patrician stock),
notorious in Syracuse for his dissipation,
in the dissipated reign of Michael the Third.

On the Ship

It certainly bears some resemblance, this small portrait,
done in pencil.

Hastily drawn right there on the ship's deck
one magical afternoon,
the Ionian Sea all around us.

It bears a resemblance. But I remember him as even more
    handsome,
more sensual, almost painfully so,
which casts his features in a more vivid light.
He seems even more handsome to me
now that my soul calls him back, out of Time.

Out of Time. All of these things are so very old –
the sketch, the ship, that afternoon.

Of Demetrius Soter (162–150 BC)

All of his hopes had come to naught!

He had imagined deeds of great renown,
ridding his homeland of the humiliation
that rankled since the battle of Magnesia.
He imagined Syria again a formidable power,
with her armies and her fleets,
with impregnable castles, and great wealth.

In Rome he suffered, growing bitter
at the conversation of friends, the youth
of the great houses of that city,
who showed such tact and courtesy to him,
the son of the great King Seleucus
Philopator – bitter at what he thought was their secret
contempt for the Hellenizing dynasties,
believing them obsolete, unfit for any real undertaking,
totally incapable of governing their own people.
He'd sit apart, fume alone and swear
the way they saw things would not long stand;
just look at his determination;
he will strive, he will act and rise up.

If only he could make his way to the East,
be free of Italy finally –
then all of the dynamism
in his soul, all of that initiative,
he would transmit to his people.

Ah, if only he might find himself in Syria!
He was so young when he'd fled his homeland
that he barely remembered her.
But in his mind he dwelt on her always,
as if it were some holy icon approached only in pilgrimage,
the dream of a beautiful landscape, a vision
of Greek cities and Greek harbours.

And now?
Despair and helpless longing.
They were right, those youths in Rome.
The dynasties that rose from the Macedonian conquests
were unsustainable.

No matter: he did his best;
he fought as long as he could.
But in his dark chagrin
there is one thing alone that he still contemplates
with pride: that even in this, his failure,
he showed the same indomitable bravery to the world.

As for the rest – they were mere dreams and futile diversions.
And Syria – it almost doesn't seem like his homeland any
      more;
now it's the land of Balas and Heracleides.

If Indeed Dead

'Where was he off to, where did the sage disappear?
After that string of miracles, after the repute of his teaching
had spread to so many lands, suddenly he hid himself away,
and no one ever learned with certainty what had happened
(no one ever identified his grave).
Some spread the rumour that he'd died in Ephesus.
But Damis never wrote about that; nothing
about Apollonius' death did Damis ever relay.
Others said he'd disappeared at Lindos.
Or perhaps that other story is true,
the one about his ascension in Crete,
in the ancient sanctuary of Dictynna.
But then we have his wondrous,
divine apparition before the young student in Tyana.
Perhaps the time isn't right for his return,
for his reappearance in this world;
or maybe he has merely altered his form
and he wanders among us unrecognized.
But he'll appear again, just as he once was,
to show us the way. Then, surely,
he'll restore the worship of our gods,
and our elegant Hellenic rituals.'

Thus daydreamed one of the minority pagans,
one of the few that remained,
lounging in his meagre apartment after reading
Philostratus' biography of Apollonius of Tyana.
Otherwise the man was a nothing, a faint-heart
who in public played the Christian
and made appearances in church.
This during the reign of Justin the Elder,
who ruled in strictest piety
when Alexandria, then a god-fearing city,
abhorred wretched idolaters.

Young Men of Sidon (AD 400)

The actor they had hired to entertain the group
also declaimed a few choice epigrams.

The room opened on to the garden;
a delicate fragrance of flowers
fused with the aroma
of the five perfumed young men of Sidon.

Meleager was read, then Crinagoras, and Rhianus.
But when the actor recited the lines
'Aeschylus lies here, son of Euphorion, an Athenian –'
(emphasizing perhaps a bit too strongly
the phrases 'martial strength' and 'Marathon grove'),
one fiery young lad, wild about literature,
leaped up and shouted:

'I don't like that quatrain in the least.
Comments like that show a failure of nerve.
I say devote all of your strength to your oeuvre,
all of your care and effort.
And in times of hardship, or when your hour is near,
it's your work you must remember.
This is what I expect and what I demand.
Do not cast from your mind
the brilliant language of Tragedy –
the *Agamemnon*, the wondrous *Prometheus*,
the characters of Orestes and Cassandra,
the *Seven Against Thebes* – and then claim as your record
    on earth
only the fact that you stood in the army's ranks,
and that you too, amid the masses, fought Datis and
    Artaphernes.'

That They May Come

One candle will suffice.   The gentle light it gives
suits the ambience better,   makes the room more alluring
for the Shades of Love,   whenever they may come.

One candle will suffice.   The room tonight
should have very faint light.   For deep in reverie
and suggestiveness –   in the softest light –
I will conjure my visions,   lost in feeling,
so the shades may come,   the Shades of Love.

Darius

The poet Phernazes is labouring
over the critical passage in his epic:
the manner in which Darius, son of Hystaspes,
acquired the kingdom of the Persians (it's from Darius, of
    course,
that our own glorious king, Mithridates,
Dionysus and Eupator, is descended).
But here philosophy is required: the poet must analyse
the emotions that spurred King Darius –
was it arrogance perhaps, and intoxication? No, more likely
it was a clear understanding of the vanity of greatness.
It is a question the poet ponders at length.

But suddenly a servant rushes in, interrupting
his train of thought, to announce the momentous news:
war with Rome has begun;
the greater part of our army has crossed the borders.

The poet sits in shock. What unfortunate timing!
How will Mithridates, Dionysus and Eupator,
our glorious king, give his attention now to Greek poems?
In time of war – just imagine, Greek poems of all things!

Phernazes is anxious. What terrible luck!
Just when he had some hope with his new *Darius*
to win the acclaim he'd sought, to finally silence
his envious critics. But now, what delay,
what a postponement to his plans.

And if it were merely a delay, all well and good.
But are we even safe here in Amisos?
The town is not very well fortified
and the Romans are the most frightening of enemies.

Do we really have any hope of standing against them,
we Cappadocians? Is it even possible?
How are we to measure up against their legions?
Great gods, protectors of Asia, come to our aid.

Yet, amid all of this turbulence and misfortune,
the poetic idea keeps revolving insistently –
surely it was arrogance and intoxication;
it was arrogance and intoxication that drove Darius.

Anna Comnena

In the prologue of her *Alexiad*
Anna Comnena laments her widowhood.

Her soul is awhirl. 'And with rivers of tears,' she tells us,
'I bathe my eyes ... in sorrow for the tempests' of her life,
'sorrow for the insurrections' she faced. The grief burns
'in the very marrow of my bone, in the rending of my soul'.

But the truth is there was but one grief
that this ambitious lady ever knew;
only one profound regret did she feel,
this haughty Greek lady (even though she will not admit it):
she never managed, for all her cunning,
to take possession of the empire. She watched as it was taken,
snatched from her very hands, by the insolent John.

Byzantine Aristocrat, in Exile, Composing Verses

Let the frivolous call me frivolous.
In serious matters I was always most attentive.
And I assure you, there is no one
with a better knowledge of the Holy Fathers, the Scriptures
or the Canons of the Synods than myself.
For whenever Botaniates was in doubt,
whenever he stumbled on some ecclesiastical question,
it was me he'd consult, me before all others.
But now, exiled here (thanks to that busybody Irene Ducas,
may she rot), suffering the most dreadful boredom,
it's no disgrace if I distract myself
by writing sextains and octets –
or amuse myself with mythological tales
of Hermes and Apollo and Dionysus,
or the heroes of Thessaly and the Peloponnese,
or spend hours polishing my iambics,
iambics so correct that – if I may say so – even the learned
clerics of Constantinople could not match them.
It's their very perfection that provokes such censure.

Their Beginning

The fulfilling of their lawless pleasures
now complete, they rise from the bed
and hurriedly dress without speaking.
They emerge separately, furtively from the house,
and as they walk somewhat uneasily down the street,
it appears they suspect something about them betrays
the sort of bed they fell upon just a moment ago.

But what great profit to the artist's life:
tomorrow, the day after, or years later, he'll write
the powerful lines that had their beginning here.

The Favourite of Alexander Balas

I'm not angry the chariot wheel broke
or that I lost the race – that joke.
I'll spend the night drinking fine wines
amid wreaths of beautiful roses. All Antioch is mine.
I am the most talked about youth here.
I am Balas's singular weakness, the one he most adores.
Tomorrow, just wait, they'll say the race was rigged.
(But if I'd arranged it in secret, if I were truly without taste –
they'd even say my crippled chariot came first, the flatterers.)

The Melancholy of Jason Cleander,
Poet in Commagene, AD 595

The ageing of my body and my face
is a wound from a merciless knife.
I can endure it no longer.
So I turn to you, Poetic Art,
for you know something about remedies;
experiments to quiet the pain, through Fantasy and Language.

It's a wound from a merciless knife.
Bring your remedies, Poetic Art,
that remove – for a while – any awareness of injury.

Demaratus

His chosen theme: The Character of Demaratus.
Porphyry had suggested it in conversation
and the young sophist prepared a preliminary sketch
(with the aim of developing it rhetorically later).

'A courtier first of the Persian King Darius,
and later of King Xerxes;
now, travelling with Xerxes and his army,
Demaratus would finally be vindicated.

'A great injustice had been done him.
He *was* the son of Ariston. His enemies,
shamelessly, had bribed the oracle.
But they weren't satisfied with having deprived him
of his kingdom: when he surrendered and resigned himself
to living as a private citizen,
they had to go further and insult him before the people,
they had to humiliate him publicly at the festival.

'As a result, he zealously gave his support to Xerxes.
Now he will make his return to Sparta
in the company of the vast Persian army;
when he is king once more, he will quickly cast them out.
How he will shame the scheming Leotychides!

'But his days are filled with worry
as he offers guidance to the Persians, explaining
the path they must take to conquer Greece.

'He has many worries, many thoughts, and for this reason
the time passes slowly for Demaratus.
He has many worries, many thoughts, and for this reason
Demaratus has hardly a moment of joy;
for it is not joy that he feels
(it is not; he will not accept it);
how can he call it joy, when his misfortune is cresting,
when it becomes clear
that the Greeks will emerge the victors?'

I Have Brought to Art

I sit and wonder.   Longings and sensations
I have brought to Art –   faces and limbs
half glimpsed,   vague memories
of unconsummated passions.   Let me give myself to Her.
For Art knows how   to fashion the true shape of Beauty,
almost imperceptibly   completing life,
mingling impressions,   melding the days.

From the School of the Renowned Philosopher

He studied with Ammonius Saccas for two years,
but grew bored of both philosophy and Saccas.

Later he went into politics,
but gave that up too – the Eparch was a numbskull,
and his staff were all officious, formal dolts,
with the most miserable, barbaric Greek.

The church aroused his curiosity for a while;
to be baptized and live as a Christian.
But he quickly discarded that notion.
That would surely ruin things with his parents,
who flaunted their paganism.
They would immediately stop payment – horrid thought –
of his rather generous allowance.

Yet he had to do something. So he became a regular
at the houses of ill repute throughout Alexandria,
at every secret den of depravity.

For this career he seemed particularly well suited:
he had been graced with a most handsome body
and took great pleasure in the sublime gift.

For ten more years at least
his beauty would endure. Afterwards –
perhaps he'd go back to Saccas again.
And if the old man should die in the meantime,
he'd go to another philosopher;
there was always someone to be found.

Or in the end it's possible he could return
to politics – keeping most admirably in mind
the traditions of his family, his duty
to the fatherland, and similar high-sounding platitudes.

Craftsman of Wine Bowls

On this wine bowl   of pure silver –
destined for the home   of Heracleides,
where discerning taste   and elegance reside –
I've engraved flowers,   streams and thyme,
and in their midst   a handsome youth,
naked and erotic,   dangling his leg
in the water still.   I prayed, memory,
that I'd find in you   an ally strong enough to render
the face of this youth,   whom I loved, just as it once was.
It will not be easy,   as it has been
some fifteen years   from the day he fell,
a soldier,   in the battle of Magnesia.

For Those Who Fought in the Achaean League

You who fought and valiantly fell are brave beyond compare,
with no fear of enemies who were everywhere victorious.
You are yourselves blameless; but Critolaus and Diaeus are
    not.
Whenever the Greeks shall have cause to boast
they will say, 'These are the men our nation breeds,'
so splendid will be their praise of you.

Written in Alexandria by an Achaean,
in the seventh year of Ptolemy Lathyrus.

To Antiochus Epiphanes

The young Antiochian   declared to the king:
'Within my heart pulses   a cherished hope:
that the Macedonians,   Antiochus Epiphanes,
the Macedonians   will resume the great struggle.
If they should only win –   I would gladly part
with the lions and horses,   the Pan crafted in coral,
the elegant palace   and the Tyrian gardens,
all that you've given me,   Antiochus Epiphanes.'

This may have moved   the king, somewhat.
But then he remembered   his father and brother,
and held back his response.   Some eavesdropper
might hear and spread a rumour.   In any case, it ended,
as expected, horribly   and quick, at Pydna.

In an Old Book

In an antique book – about a hundred years old –
I found a watercolour sandwiched amid the pages,
totally forgotten, with no signature.
You could see it was the work of a skilful artist;
it bore the title: 'Representation of Love'.

But it should have been 'love of the most extreme
    voluptuaries'.

For it was clear when you looked at the work
(the intent of the artist was easily grasped)
that the boy in this painting was not intended
for those who love in any healthy way,
who remain within the bounds of what is normally
    permitted –
his deep, chestnut eyes, the exquisite beauty
of his face, his idealized lips that bring
such pleasure to the beloved's body;
those ideal limbs fashioned for the sort of activity
the current morality would call shameless.

In Despair

He's lost him for good,   and now on the lips
of each new lover   he seeks the lips
of the one he lost;   in every embrace
with each new lover   he tries to believe
that he's giving himself   to the same young man.

He's lost him for good,   as if he'd never existed.
The boy wished – so he said –   he wished to be freed
from the stigma and reproach   of that unhealthy pleasure;
from the stigma and reproach   of that shameful pleasure.
It wasn't too late – he said –   for him to break free.

He's lost him for good,   as if he'd never existed.
Through imagination,   and self-delusion,
he seeks those lips   on the lips of others;
he's trying to feel   that lost love again.

Julian, Seeing the Contempt

'Seeing, therefore, the great contempt
in which we hold the gods,' he says with such a serious air.
Contempt? What did he expect?
Let him reorganize the religion as he likes.
Let him counsel the High Priest of Galatia
or other such men, exhorting and directing them.
His friends were not Christians, that much was certain.
Unlike him (a Christian born and bred)
they would never aspire to dabble
in the formation of a newfangled church,
as ludicrous in concept as in application.
They were Greeks after all. Remember, Augustus –
nothing in excess.

Epitaph of Antiochus, King of Commagene

After returning from the funeral in deepest sorrow,
the sister of that restrained and gentle man,
the most learned King of Commagene, Antiochus,
desired that a fitting epitaph be composed.
Callistratus, an Ephesian sophist and frequent resident
within the narrow borders of Commagene, one who received
repeated and cordial hospitality in the royal palace,
wrote one at the suggestion of several Syrians in the court,
and sent it to the aged queen.

'People of Commagene, let the glory of Antiochus,
our beneficent king, be duly celebrated.
A judicious governor of this land,
he was a just, wise and noble leader.
But he was also that best of things: a Hellene –
beyond which mankind has no nobler attribute;
anything greater is reserved for the gods.'

Theatre of Sidon (AD 400)

The son of an upright citizen –   essentially a handsome
young man of the theatre   with varied and appealing
                                               traits.

Sometimes I compose,   in the Greek tongue,
rather bold verses,   which I then circulate,
in secret of course –   heaven forbid they be seen
by those grey prudes   who pontificate about virtue –
for these verses describe   a special kind of pleasure
and a love without issue   which is widely condemned.

Julian in Nicomedia

Pointless matters and full of risk
are these paeans to the Greek ideals,

the interest in theurgic acts, the visits to pagan temples,
this enthusiasm for the ancient gods,

his frequent chats with Chrysanthius and the theorizing
of the philosopher Maximus – admittedly a clever man.

Just look at the outcome: Gallus seems
very concerned; Constantius has suspicions.

Ah, his counsellors weren't prudent in their advice.
The whole incident – Mardonius says – has gone too far,

the tumult must be stopped at once.
So, once again, Julian returns as lector

to the church at Nicomedia. There,
in ringing tones and all due reverence,

he reads from the Holy Scriptures, and the people
stand amazed at his Christian piety.

Before Time Could Change Them

They wept horribly   at the separation.
Neither had wished it;   it was circumstance,
the need to earn a living,   where one or the other was
                                        obliged
to go far away –   New York or Canada.
Yet at that point their love   was no longer what it had
                                        been.
Their old attraction   had diminished by degrees;
their old attraction   had diminished a good deal.
But neither desired   to be split apart.
It was circumstance, surely.   Or perhaps Destiny itself
was working now as an artist,   separating them at the
                                        point
when their passion subsided,   before time could change
                                        them;
and each to the other   would remain always as he was:
a handsome young man   of twenty-four.

He Came to Read

He came to read; two or three books
are lying open: history and poetry.
But after just ten minutes of reading
he lets them drop. There on the sofa
he falls asleep. He truly is devoted to reading –
but he is twenty-three years old, and very handsome.
And just this afternoon, Eros surged
within his perfect limbs and on his lips.
Into his beautiful flesh came the heat of passion,
and there was no foolish embarrassment
about the form that pleasure took . . .

The Year 31 BC in Alexandria

From his small village on the city's outskirts,
powdered in dust from the journey,

the peddler arrived. 'Frankincense' and 'gum',
'the finest oil' and 'perfumes for your hair'

he cries through the streets. But amid the tumult,
the bands playing and the parades, he can't be heard.

He is bumped, jostled by the crowds until,
totally confused, he asks, 'What is this madness?'

Then someone tosses him the palace's gigantic lie —
that Antony is victorious in Greece.

John Cantacuzenus Has the Upper Hand

He looks out and gazes at the fields he still owns,
the wheat, the livestock and the trees
laden with fruit. Further in the distance, his ancestral home,
full of clothing, expensive furniture, fine silver.

They will take it from him – Christ! – they will take it all
    now.

Perhaps Cantacuzenus might show some mercy
if he threw himself at his feet. He's a lenient man, they say,
very lenient. But what of those around him? The army?
Perhaps I should prostrate myself in tears before Lady Irene.

Fool! To get involved with Anna's scheming –
would that King Andronicus hadn't lived
to crown her! Have we seen any good
come from that woman, have we seen any humanity?
Even the Franks no longer have any respect for her.
Her plans were laughable; her preparations utter stupidity.
While they went on threatening the people in Constantinople,
Cantacuzenus destroyed them all, Lord John destroyed them.

And to think he had planned to side with Lord John!
He would have done it too. He'd be a happier man now,
a great gentleman, well established,
if only the bishop hadn't persuaded him at the last minute,
with that imposing sacerdotal way of his,
with his information, flawed from end to end,
with his promises, and his stupidity.

Temethus, Antiochian, AD 400

Verses by the young Temethus,   wildly in love.
They bear the title 'Emonides',   who was the favoured
                         companion
of Antiochus Epiphanes,   an incredibly handsome youth,
originally from Samosata.   But if the lines have any
                         warmth
or prompt any real emotion,   it is because that name,
                         Emonides
(dating from the period,   so long ago, the year
one hundred and thirty-seven   of the Greek kingdom,
and perhaps even earlier),   was used in the poem
simply as cover,   though it was well chosen.
In fact, the poem describes   one of Temethus' own loves,
                         beautiful
and worthy in his own right.   We alone, the initiated,
his closest friends,   we, the initiated
alone know for whom   the lines were composed.
The foolish Antiochians   read only 'Emonides'.

Of Coloured Glass

I am quite touched by one detail
in the coronation, at Blachernai, of John Cantacuzenus
and Irene, daughter of Andronicus Asan.
Because they had only a few precious stones
(the poverty of our wretched kingdom being so great)
they wore artificial gems: hundreds of pieces made of glass,
red, green and blue. There is nothing
base or undignified, in my view,
about these little bits
of coloured glass. On the contrary, they seem
like a sorrowful protest
against the undeserved misfortunes of the crown.
They are the symbols of what should have been worn,
of what, assuredly, ought to have been worn
at the coronation of Lord John Cantacuzenus
and his Lady Irene, daughter of Andronicus Asan.

In the Twenty-fifth Year of His Life

He goes nightly to the saloon
where they'd met the month before.
He made inquiries, but they could tell him nothing.
From what little they'd said, he knew he'd met up
with an entirely unknown subject:
one of the many suspicious, shadowy
young forms who frequented that spot.
Yet he goes to the tavern every night
and sits there watching the entrance,
doggedly watching the entrance.
Perhaps he'll come. Perhaps tonight he'll come.

For three weeks he repeats the ritual.
His mind grows sick with lust.
Kisses linger on his lips.
Every inch of his flesh is wracked by longing.
He feels that body's touch all over.
He longs to embrace him again.

He tries, of course, not to betray his emotions.
But sometimes he is almost beyond caring.
Besides, he is well aware of the risk;
he's made up his mind. It's not improbable that this life he
     leads
will expose him to some ruinous scandal.

On Italy's Coast

Menedoros' son, Kimos,   a Greek-Italian youth,
spends his days indulging   in varied amusements,
as do many of the youth   of Magna Graecia,
brought up surrounded   by so much wealth.

But today, in contrast   to his nature, he seems
thoughtful and downcast.   Standing on the coast,
in deep distress,   he watches as they unload
the ships with their fresh   spoils from the Peloponnese.

Greek booty;   the loot of Corinth.

No, this day surely   it would be improper,
it would be impossible   for the Greek-Italian youth
to show any interest   in such pastimes.

The Dreary Village

In the dreary village where he works –
an assistant in one of the commercial establishments,
and quite young – he waits
for two or three months to pass,
for two or three months when business might slow
and he could leave for the city, to plunge straight
into the hurly-burly and amusement there;
in the dreary village where he waits –
he fell into bed tonight in a fit of passion,
all of his youth burning with carnal desire,
all of his beautiful youth in its beautiful intensity.
And in his sleep, pleasure came upon him; in his sleep
he sees and holds those limbs, the flesh he desired . . .

Apollonius of Tyana in Rhodes

Apollonius was concluding his discourse
on proper education and comportment
to a young man then building
a luxurious residence in Rhodes: 'For example,
I would much rather see upon entering a temple,
however small it may be,
a statue made of gold and ivory,
than find in a large temple
a common figure made of clay.'

The 'common' and the 'clay' – what an abomination! –
and yet some (those without sufficient training)
are easily fooled by the lie: the common and the clay.

The Illness of Cleitus

Cleitus, an attractive young man
around twenty-three years of age –
with the finest upbringing and a rare command of Greek –
is gravely ill. The fever which this year
swept all Alexandria has afflicted him as well.

The fever took him when he was already worn down,
grieving over the loss of his companion, a young actor
who had ceased to love or care for him.

He is gravely ill, and his parents tremble with foreboding.

An old maidservant who helped raise Cleitus
also fears for his life.
And in her deep concern
she recalls a pagan idol she once worshipped
as a child, before she became a servant there,
in the house of such prominent Christians,
and before she became a Christian herself.
Secretly she begins to gather cakes, wine and honey.
She lays them before the idol. She chants
a half-forgotten prayer – recalling a phrase here and there.
        Poor fool,
she doesn't understand the black demon cares little
whether a Christian lives or not.

In a Town of Asia Minor

The news of the outcome of the battle of Actium
certainly took us by surprise.
Still, there's no need to draft a new proclamation.
Only the names need changing. Instead of writing
in the closing lines, 'Having delivered the Romans
from the pernicious Octavian,
that parody of a Caesar,'
we'll now write: 'Having delivered the Romans
from the pernicious Antony.'
The remainder of the text fits perfectly.

'All hail the most glorious victor,
invincible in works of war,
brilliant in all his political achievements,
on whose behalf the town prayed ardently,
for the great triumph of Antony ...'
Here, as we mentioned, we'll insert the change: 'Of Octavian,
the greatest gift of Zeus –
all hail the mighty bulwark of the Greeks,
who has the highest regard for Greek customs,
who is beloved in every region of Greece,
and deserves the loudest praise,
whose exploits demand to be recounted at length
in the Greek tongue, in both prose and verse;
in the Greek tongue, that instrument of fame,'
et cetera, et cetera. It all fits together brilliantly.

Priest at the Serapeion

For that kind old man, my dear father,
who loved me ever the same;
for that kind old man I mourn.
He died two days ago, just before dawn.

Christ, I strive every day
to keep the precepts
of your most holy church in every act
and in every word and every thought.
Anyone who would deny you, I shun. But now I lament,
I grieve, Christ, for my dear father,
who nevertheless was – how terrible to speak it! –
a priest in the accursed Serapeion.

In the Bars

I'm wallowing in the bars   and brothels of Beirut.
I had no desire   to stay in Alexandria.
Tamides has left me   for the Eparch's son,
for a villa on the Nile,   and a mansion in town.
To stay in Alexandria   wouldn't do for me.
I'm wallowing in the bars   and brothels of Beirut.
In base debauchery   I lead a dirty, sordid life.
My one consolation,   like long-lasting beauty,
like a scent that has stayed   lingering on my skin,
is that for two years I had   that most exquisite youth,
Tamides, as my own,   as my very own,
and not for a house   or a villa on the Nile.

A Great Procession of Clergy and Laymen

A great procession of clergy and laymen
with all of the guilds clearly represented
makes its way through the streets, the squares,
and under the gates of the renowned city of Antioch.
At the head of this imposing parade
stands a beautiful young boy, dressed in white,
bearing in his upraised hands the Cross,
the holy Cross, our strength and hope.
The pagans, so arrogant before,
seem reserved and timid now; they distance themselves
hastily from the procession. Let them remain
far away from us always (those who fail to renounce their
    error).
Onward proceeds the holy Cross; and in every neighbourhood
where Christians live in piety
it brings great consolation and great joy:
the pious stand at the doors of their homes
and full of exultation they bow in reverence
to the strength and salvation of the world, the Cross.

This is an annual Christian festival.
But today it is celebrated more openly, as you see.
For the state has been delivered at last.
The sacrilegious, the abominable Julian
no longer reigns.

Let us pray for Jovian, most pious of men.

Scholar Departing Syria

Respected scholar,   now that you are departing Syria
and plan to compose   a history of Antioch,
it would be worth mentioning Mebis   in the work you are
                                              planning.
For the well-known Mebis,   without question,
is the most handsome,   the most beloved young man,
in all of Antioch.   No other youth in that line of work
commands such a price.   To have Mebis as your own
for only two or three days   it was not uncommon
to pay one hundred staters.   Of course, that was in
                                              Antioch;
but even in Alexandria,   and in Rome too for that matter,
you won't easily find a young man   as alluring as Mebis.

Julian and the Antiochians

They say neither the Chi nor the Kappa had ever harmed the
city ... but having found an explanation ... we learned that
these letters are the first initials of two names, one being
Christ, and the other Constantius.

Julian, *Misopogon*

Was it possible they would ever renounce
their beautiful way of life, the rich variety
of their daily entertainments or their brilliant theatre,
where every evening they fashioned a union of Art
and the erotic tendencies of the flesh?

Yes, they were immoral, to a point – and, I suppose,
well beyond that point. But they had the consolation
that theirs was the notorious life of Antioch,
redolent of pleasure, the epitome of taste.

Renounce all that? And give heed to what?

His empty talk about false gods,
his endless rhapsodies about himself,
his childish phobia of the theatre,
his graceless priggishness and that laughable beard?

Of course they preferred the Chi.
Of course they preferred the Kappa. A hundred times more.

Anna Dalassena

In the imperial decree that Alexius Comnenus published,
apparently to pay honour to his mother,
the most wise Lady Anna Dalassena –
distinguished by her deeds and her character –
there are countless expressions of praise:
among the many let us mention
just one lovely, noble phrase:
'Neither "mine" nor "yours", those cold-hearted words, was
            ever spoken.'

Days of 1896

He is utterly disgraced.   An erotic proclivity,
quite forbidden   and widely condemned
(yet congenital nonetheless),   was the cause:
for public opinion   was terribly prudish.
Bit by bit he was deprived   of the little income he had;
then came a loss in status,   and the respect he once
                                                commanded.
He was nearing thirty   but had never gone a year
in full employment,   or at least a job he could talk about.
At times he earned   some semblance of a livelihood
by brokering meetings   considered shameful.
He ended up one of those who,   if you were seen with him
often enough, you could be   terribly compromised.

But no, that will not do;   this picture isn't right.
The memory of his beauty   deserves better than this.
There is another point of view,   and seen from that angle
he is quite appealing;   a simple and true
child of Eros who,   without hesitation,
placed far above his honour   and reputation,
the pure pleasure   that his pure flesh could give.

Above his own reputation?   But public opinion,
which was so terribly prudish,   so often got it wrong.

Two Young Men, Twenty-three to
Twenty-four Years Old

He'd been sitting at the café since half past ten,
expecting him to appear at any moment.
Midnight came and went, and he still waited.
Soon it would be one thirty; the café
was almost completely empty.
He grew tired of reading the newspapers mechanically.
Of his original three shillings
only one remained: while waiting there
he'd spent the rest on coffee and brandy.
He'd smoked all his cigarettes.
The waiting had exhausted him. Alone
all those hours, insidious thoughts began to rankle
about the wayward life he led.

But when he saw his friend arrive – at once
the fatigue, the boredom, and the dark thoughts all vanished.

His friend brought unexpected good news:
he'd won sixty pounds playing cards.

Their handsome faces, their buoyant youth,
the sensuous love they both shared
were refreshed, had come alive and were fortified
by those sixty pounds won at cards.

Now full of joy and strength, sensuousness and beauty,
they departed – not to the homes of their respectable families
(where, after all, they were no longer welcome):
but to a place known only to them, a special
establishment of vice, where they requested
a room with a bed, expensive cocktails, and started to drink
    again.

When the drinks ran dry
and it was nearing four in the morning,
they gave themselves, happy at last, to love.

Greek Since Antiquity

Antioch boasts   of her splendid buildings
and her lovely streets;   of the marvellous beauty
of her surrounding countryside   and the great multitude
of her citizens.   She boasts of being the seat
of glorious kings;   of her many artists
and wise men,   of her wealthy
and shrewd merchants.   But incomparably more
than all of these,   Antioch boasts of being a city
Greek since antiquity;   related to Argos through Ione,
and founded herself   by Argive colonists,
in an effort to honour   Inachus' daughter.

Days of 1901

This is what was so exceptional about him:
that despite all his profligacy
and his vast experience of love,
despite the fact that his comportment
matched his years perfectly,
there were moments – extremely rare
of course – when he gave the impression
that his flesh had almost never been touched.

The beauty of his twenty-nine years,
a beauty so well tested by pleasure,
could at times make one believe
he was a mere adolescent who – a bit awkwardly –
surrenders his chaste body to love for the very first time.

You Did Not Understand

Speaking of our religious beliefs –
the vacuous Julian said: 'I read, I understood,
I condemned.' As if he thought he could annihilate us
with that 'condemned' of his, the buffoon!

We Christians, however, have no truck with such cleverness.
We answered him straight away: 'You read,
but you did not understand; for if you had understood,
you would not have condemned.'

A Young Writer – in His Twenty-fourth Year

Now, brain, work as hard as you can.
A one-sided passion is wearing him thin.
He's in a state of nervous anxiety.
He kisses that adored face every day,
his hands all over those exquisite limbs.
He never loved before with so intense
a passion, but the happy fulfilment of Eros
is wanting; missing is the satisfaction that comes
when there are two who long with the same intensity.

(But these two are not equally given to their illicit passion.
It possessed only him in full.)

So he is worn down, his nerves completely frayed.
He's jobless too, which makes matters worse.
He borrows a few pounds here and there,
and with difficulty (sometimes he almost has to beg)
he just about gets by.
He kisses those lips he adores; and upon
that exquisite body – which he now knows
merely tolerates him – he takes his pleasure.
Then he drinks and smokes; drinks and smokes,
and loiters in the coffee shops all day,
tediously lugging his heart-ache for that beauty.
Now, brain, work as hard as you can.

In Sparta

King Cleomenes didn't know, he wouldn't dare –
he didn't know how to frame the words
to tell his mother: Ptolemy demanded,
as guarantee for the truce, that she be sent to Egypt
to be kept there under house arrest;
a most humiliating, a most inappropriate thing.
Time and again he verged on speaking; yet every time he
      hesitated.
Time and again he verged on telling her; yet every time he
      stopped.

But that excellent lady understood
(she'd heard the rumours already),
and prompted him to speak.
Then she laughed, and said she would certainly obey.
In fact, she would take great joy in the fact that she was able,
even at her age, to be of use to Sparta still.

As for the humiliation – she was quite indifferent to it.
It was utterly impossible for an upstart Lagid
to understand true Spartan pride.
His demand, therefore, could in no way result
in the humiliation of so eminent a lady
as herself: the mother of a Spartan king.

Picture of a Young Man of Twenty-three, Painted by His Friend of the Same Age, an Amateur

He completed the portrait   yesterday afternoon.
Now he scans it carefully: the subject is shown
in a grey jacket, dark grey,   unbuttoned, with no vest
and no tie underneath.   The shirt is pink
and left just open enough   to allow a glance
at his fine-looking chest   and his elegant neck.
The brow, on his right,   is almost completely obscured
by a curl of his hair,   that rich, thick hair
(done in the style   he wore that year).
Throughout the portrait   you see the extreme sensuousness
with which he endowed it,   when he painted the eyes,
when he drew the lips . . .   the mouth, those lips,
created for the fulfilment   of a particular pleasure.

In a Large Greek Colony, 200 BC

That things are not going well in the colony,
no one has the slightest doubt,
and although we are making some progress,
perhaps, as not a few people believe, the time has come
to bring in a Reform Politician.

The issue, however, and the difficulty,
is that they make such a big deal
of everything, these reformers.
(How fortùnate it would be
if no one ever needed them.) On every subject,
no matter how small, they make inquiries and hold counsels,
and suddenly they set their minds on radical change
which must then be accomplished without the slightest delay.

They also tend to recommend great sacrifice:

You must abandon this property;
your ownership of it presents risks:
these are the sort of properties that could most injure the
     colony.
Give up this one source of revenue,
and the other which flows from it,
and then this third one: it's a natural consequence of the
     second;
it's true, they are substantial, but what else can be done?
They constitute a painful liability for you.

And as they proceed with their investigation
they continue to unearth extraneous items they want
     eliminated;
items which, however, one finds it difficult to part with.

And when, finally, they complete their work,
when everything's been identified and reduced to the last
    detail,
and they go off, taking with them their due remuneration,
we are left behind to inventory what is left,
after such drastic surgery has been performed.

But maybe the time has not yet come.
Why be in such a rush? Haste can be such a dangerous thing.
Premature measures always bring regrets.
It's true, and regrettable, the colony has many flaws.
But what work of humankind is without blemish?
And, after all, we are making some progress.

A Prince from Western Libya

Aristomenes, son of Menelaus,
a prince from western Libya,
was generally quite well liked in Alexandria
during his ten-day sojourn there.
His attire, like his name, was decorous and clearly Greek.
He received his tributes gladly
but without seeking them out, modest as he was.
He bought a number of Greek manuscripts,
particularly those dealing with history and philosophy.
But above all he seemed a man of few words.
He was a deep thinker, or so it was rumoured,
and such men, by nature, tend not to speak at length.

In fact, he was not deep in his thinking or in anything else.
He was an ordinary, ridiculous man.
He took a Greek name, dressed in Greek fashions,
and studied how to comport himself like a Greek;
all the while he shuddered to think he might spoil
the tolerably good impression he'd made
by blurting out some truly barbaric solecisms.
Then the Alexandrians would mock him
in their usual way, merciless people that they are.

And so he confined himself to just a few words,
taking great care to get his declensions and accents right;
and he suffered no little pain in the struggle to keep
so much talk pent up within him.

Cimon, Son of Learchos, Twenty-two Years of Age, Student of Greek Literature (in Cyrene)

'Death came to me   when I was still happy,
for Hermoteles and I   were still inseparably close.
Through my final days,   though he pretended
to appear unconcerned   I often noticed his eyes
welling with tears.   Whenever he thought
I had fallen asleep   he would collapse, distraught,
on the edge of my bed.   We were young,
identical in age,   both twenty-three years old.
Yet Fate loves to betray us.   Some fresh passion, perhaps,
could have captured Hermoteles   and taken him from me.
But I ended things well   in a love still undivided.'

I received this epitaph,   written for Marylus, son of
                                                Aristodemus,
who died a month ago   in Alexandria. In mourning
I received it,   for I am Cimon, his cousin.
The poet who wrote and sent it   was an acquaintance of
                                                mine.
He sent it because   he recalled that in some way
I was related to Marylus: that was all he knew.
My soul is now full   of sorrow for Marylus.
We had grown up together   and were close as brothers.
I am deeply saddened.   His premature death
has extinguished completely   any rancour I felt,
any grudge that I had   against young Marylus –
for he once stole away the love   Hermoteles had for me.
But now, even if Hermoteles   should want me back
it would never be the same.   I know my character,
the frailties I possess.   The image of Marylus
would come between us;   I would hear him saying:
'There you are,   I see you're satisfied now.
Look at how you've won him back,   just as you'd always
                                                hoped, Cimon;
at least you have no cause   for slandering me now.'

On the March to Sinope

Mithridates, famous and mighty,
master of great cities,
commander of vast armies and fleets,
took an out-of-the-way route on the march to Sinope,
quite remote, where a fortune-teller made his home.

Mithridates ordered one of his officers
to ask the soothsayer how much more wealth he would
    acquire in the future,
how much more power.

He ordered one of his officers and then
continued on his way to Sinope.

The soothsayer retreated to his secret den.
About thirty minutes later he emerged,
careworn, and spoke to the officer:
'I am unable to interpret the vision to my satisfaction.
The day is not propitious.
I saw several shadowy matters, but could not construe them
    properly.
But the king should remain content, I think, with what he
    now possesses.
Anything more could be dangerous.
Remember to tell him that, officer:
may he remain content, by god, with what he has!
Fortune takes sudden turns.
Tell King Mithridates this:
all too rarely does one find a man like his ancestor's
    companion,
that noble friend who, just in time, turned his spear-point
to the ground to write those life-saving words: *Run,*
    Mithridates.'

Days of 1909, 1910 and 1911

The son of a put-upon, dirt-poor sailor
(from some island in the Aegean),
he worked as a blacksmith's apprentice. He had rags
for clothes, his pitiful working boots were in tatters,
his hands filthy with rust and oil.

In the evening, when the shop closed,
if there were something he especially wanted,
a necktie with a rather high price-tag,
a necktie to wear on Sundays,
or if he caught a glimpse of a nice blue shirt
in the shop window and hankered after it,
he'd sell his body for a shilling or two.

I wonder if Alexandria, in all its glory, in all the long history
of its ancient days, had ever seen a youth more exquisite,
more perfect than this boy – who went utterly to waste.
For, of course, no statue or portrait
was ever made. Stuck there in that grimy blacksmith's shop,
worn down by the wrack and strain of work,
and by the working man's rough pleasures, the boy went
     quickly to ruin.

Myres: Alexandria, AD 340

When I learned the news of Myres' death,
I went straight to his house, though generally
I avoid entering the homes of Christians,
especially at times of celebration or mourning.

I stood in the entrance hall. I had no desire
to proceed any further; I was aware
that the relatives of the deceased were staring
with obvious surprise and displeasure.

They had put him in a large room
and from the corner where I stood I only
caught a glimpse: expensive carpets everywhere,
and decorative vessels made of gold and silver.

I stood and wept in that corner of the hall.
I started thinking how, without Myres, our parties
and excursions would be pointless now;
I imagined how it would be, no longer seeing him
at those elegant, indecent all-night affairs
enjoying himself and laughing, reciting verses
with that perfect feel for Greek rhythm that he had;
I was thinking about how I had lost his beauty
forever, how I had lost forever
the youth I had adored so passionately.

Some elderly women beside me were talking
in hushed tones about his final day –
how he kept mouthing the name 'Christ',
how his hands had gripped the cross.
Then four Christian priests entered his room,
chanting prayers and making supplication
to Jesus, or maybe it was Mary
(I'm not very familiar with their religion).

We all knew, of course, that Myres was a Christian.
We knew it from the moment we met,
when he joined our group two years ago.
But still he lived just as we did. If anything,
he was more pleasure-prone than the rest of us,
spending money lavishly on fun and games.
He was indifferent to the judgements of others,
and whenever our group happened upon
some rival crew, he threw himself
eagerly into those night-time brawls.
He never would talk about his religion.
One time we even said
we'd take him with us to the Serapeion.
But he was not pleased with that little joke
of ours: I remember now.
And yes, now I recall two other occasions:
once, when we poured libations to Poseidon
he retreated from our circle and turned his gaze away.
And when one of us excitedly said:
'May we all be granted the favour and protection
of the great, the beautiful Apollo', Myres whispered
(the others didn't hear him): 'All except me.'

The Christian priests with their droning voices
went on praying for the young man's soul.
I noticed with how much diligence,
with what careful attention, they carried out
the formalities of their faith, as they continued
the preparations for the Christian funeral.
And suddenly an odd sensation came over me: I felt
in some vague way that Myres was abandoning me;
I felt he had been united now, a Christian,
with his own people, and that I was becoming
a *stranger*, a *total stranger*. I felt another doubt

coming on as well: perhaps I'd been deceived
by my passion, perhaps I'd been a stranger to him always.
Suddenly I had to run from that dreadful home,
I had to flee before my memory of Myres
was kidnapped and corrupted by their Christianity.

Alexander Jannaeus and Alexandra

Pleased with themselves and filled with success,
King Alexander Jannaeus
and his consort, Queen Alexandra,
pass along the streets of Jerusalem
with every conceivable luxury and splendour,
a flourish of music before them.
Clearly it has come to a brilliant end,
the work begun by the great Judas Maccabeus
and his four illustrious siblings;
the work that had continued unremittingly
amid so many dangers and hardships.
Now nothing inappropriate remained.
There was no further subjection to the arrogant
sovereigns of Antioch. For now, behold,
King Alexander Jannaeus
and his consort, Queen Alexandra,
are the peers of the Seleucids in every respect.
Good Jews, pure Jews, faithful Jews – this above all –
yet, as circumstances required,
conversant also in the Greek tongue,
maintaining relations with the Greeks
and the Hellenizing monarchs – but as equals, let it be known.
Yes, indeed, it has succeeded brilliantly:
it has come to such a splendid, such a distinguished
        conclusion,
the work begun by the great Judas Maccabeus
and his four illustrious siblings.

Lovely Flowers, White Ones, That Matched So Well

He entered the café   they used to frequent together.
It was here that his friend   three months ago had said:
'We haven't a farthing between us.   We're utterly broke.
There's nothing left   but loitering in cheap taverns.
I'm telling you straight,   I can't afford to be with you.
Someone else, you know,   is interested in me now.'
This other had promised him   two suits and a few
silk handkerchiefs.   To get him to come back
he searched everywhere   and found twenty pounds.
For twenty pounds,   his friend returned;
but beyond that, surely,   he returned for their friendship,
for the love they shared,   the deep feeling between them.
The other one had lied,   he was a nasty piece of work;
he'd only placed one suit   on order for him, and that
only grudgingly,   after a thousand requests.

But now he no longer   has any desire for the suit,
he has no desire   for silk handkerchiefs,
or twenty pounds,   or even twenty pence.

They buried him on Sunday,   at ten in the morning.
They buried him on Sunday,   a week ago now.

And on the cheap coffin   he laid some flowers,
lovely flowers, white ones,   that matched so well
his youthful beauty,   his twenty-two years.

When he went in the evening   to the same café
they used to frequent together –   he happened to find
                                                              work;
he still had to earn a living –   that dark café
they used to frequent together   was like a knife in his
                                                              heart.

Come, O King of the Lacedaemonians

Cratesiclea would not condescend
to let the world see her weep or lament;
she walked majestically and in silence.
Her tranquil countenance showed no sign
of the sorrow and torment she felt within.
But even so, for a moment she lost her self-control;
before embarking on that wretched ship
that would take her to Alexandria, she escorted her son to
    Poseidon's sanctuary,
and when they were alone she saw that he was,
as Plutarch says, 'anguished' and 'shaken
with terror', so she kissed and embraced him.
Then her indomitable character prevailed
and, coming to herself, the admirable woman
addressed Cleomenes: 'Come, O King
of the Lacedaemonians, and once outside,
let none see us weep or behave in any way
unworthy of Sparta.
That alone is within our power; as for success
or disappointment, those wait on us as the deity decrees.'

Then she stepped on to the ship, bound for whatever is
    'decreed'.

In the Same Space

This setting of houses and cafés, the neighbourhood
where I gaze and where I stroll, for years and years.

I have fashioned you in joy and in sorrow,
through so many happenings, out of so many things.

You've been wholly transformed into feeling, for me.

The Mirror in the Entrance Hall

In the entrance hall of the elegant home
stood a large mirror, very old,
acquired at least eighty years ago.

A handsome youth, a tailor's apprentice
(on Sundays an amateur athlete),
was standing with a package. He handed it
to someone at the door who took it inside;
then he waited for the receipt. The tailor's apprentice
remained alone and waited.
He approached the mirror, gazed at his reflection
and straightened his tie. Five minutes later
they came with the receipt. He took it and left.

But the old mirror that during all the many years
of its existence had looked upon
thousands of objects and faces,
the old mirror was happy now,
filled with the satisfaction that it had received,
if only for a few minutes, beauty in all its perfection.

He Asked About the Quality

From the office where he'd been taken on
to fill a position that was trivial and poorly paid
(eight pounds a month, including bonus) –
he emerged as soon as he'd finished the dreary tasks
that kept him bent over his desk all afternoon.
At seven he came out and began to stroll
slowly down the street. He was handsome
in an interesting way, with the look of a man
who had reached the peak of his sensual potential.
He'd turned twenty-nine a month before.

He dawdled along the street, then down
the shabby alleys that led to his apartment.

As he passed a little shop that sold cheap
imitation goods for workmen,
inside he saw a face, a physique
that urged him on, and in he walked,
inquiring about some coloured handkerchiefs.

He asked about the quality of the handkerchiefs
and what they cost; his voice
breaking, almost stifled by desire.
The answers came back in the same tone,
distracted, the low timbre
suggesting veiled consent.

They went on talking about the merchandise –
but their sole aim was for their hands to touch
over the handkerchiefs, for their faces,
their lips, as if by chance, to brush against each other:
for some momentary contact of the flesh.

Swiftly and in secret, so that the shop owner,
seated at the back, would never notice.

They Should Have Taken the Time

Here I am destitute, almost homeless.
This fatal city, Antioch,
has swallowed all my cash;
this fatal city with its high cost of living.

Yet I'm still young and in excellent health.
My command of Greek is superb
(I know Aristotle and Plato backwards,
orators, poets – whatever you like),
I am somewhat versed in military matters,
and have connections to all the right mercenary leaders.
I am also well positioned for an administrative post.
I stayed six months in Alexandria last year
and have some acquaintance (this too is useful) with matters
    there:
the schemes of the Malefactor, the swindles, and the rest.

Therefore I believe I am abundantly qualified
to be of service in some way to this country,
to my dear fatherland, Syria.

In whatever work they set me to I will strive
to do some good for the country. That is my intention.
But if they get in my way with their idiocies –
we know the scoundrels: need we name names?
If they get in my way, it isn't my fault.

I will approach Zabinas first,
And if the fool doesn't recognize my talents,
I will go to his rival, to Grypus.
And if that idiot does not take me on,
I'll make my way straight to Hyrcanus.

One of the three is bound to want me.

My conscience is clear
regarding the indifference of my choice.
For the three of them do just about equal harm to Syria.

It's not my fault, ruined as I am.
I'm only trying, in my misfortune, to patch something
     together.
The almighty gods should have taken the time
to create a fourth man, a good one.
I would gladly have gone to work for him.

Following the Recipes of Ancient
Greco-Syrian Magicians

'What extract can be distilled
from magic herbs,' the voluptuary asked,
'what extract, following the recipes
of ancient Greco-Syrian magicians that,
for the span of a day (if its potency lasts
no longer), or even a few hours,
can bring back my twenty-third year,
and with it my friend of twenty-two –
his beauty, and his love?

'What extract can be distilled following the recipes
of ancient Greco-Syrian magicians that,
along with this recaptured past,
could bring back also that little room?'

In the Year 200 BC

'Alexander, son of Philip, and the Hellenes, all except the
    Lacedaemonians –'

One can very well imagine how completely
indifferent they must have been in Sparta
regarding that inscription: 'All except the Lacedaemonians.'
Naturally. The Spartans are not the sort
to be led by others, ordered about
like precious servants. Besides,
a Panhellenic expedition
without a Spartan king as leader
would not have appeared to them a very serious undertaking.
Assuredly: 'All except the Lacedaemonians.'

That is one perspective. It's understood.

And thus, without the Lacedaemonians at Granicus;
then again at Issus; and then in the final battle
where the dreaded army was swept away,
the host that the Persians had gathered at Arbela,
that set out for victory, and was swept away.

And from this amazing Panhellenic expedition,
victorious, splendid, renowned,
glorified as none before it,
this incomparable expedition – from it we have emerged:
a great new Hellenic world.

We, the Alexandrians, the men of Antioch,
the Seleucians, and the numberless
Greeks of Egypt and of Syria,
and those in Media and in Persia, and all the rest.
With our extensive dominions,
and the wealth of influence due to our judicious policies,
and our Common Greek Language,
which we carried all the way to Bactria, even to the Indians.

Talk about the Lacedaemonians now!

Days of 1908

That year he found himself out of work,
and so he made a living playing cards
or backgammon, and from whatever he could borrow.

He'd been offered work at a small stationer's
for three pounds a month.
Without a second thought he turned it down.
It wouldn't do. That was no salary for him,
a young man of twenty-five,
with a decent education.

He made – or failed to make – two or three shillings a day.
What else could a youth expect to win at cards
or backgammon in the sort of working-class cafés he
      frequented,
no matter how skilfully he played, or how stupid his
      opponents?
As for the loans, that was even worse.
On rare occasions he got a crown. More often, half.
Sometimes just a shilling.

When he was able to escape the grim, nightly ritual
for a week, or sometimes longer,
he would go and freshen up at the baths, with a morning
      swim.

His clothes were in terrible disrepair.
He wore the same suit all the time,
a faded cinnamon-coloured suit.

Ah, days of summer, nineteen hundred and eight,
your vision of him, for beauty's sake,
omitted that faded cinnamon-coloured suit.

Instead, your vision preserved him
just as he was taking it off, casting away
that unworthy clothing, and the mended underwear,
and he stood completely naked, flawless in his beauty; a
    miracle.
His hair uncombed, tossed back,
his limbs lightly tanned
from those naked mornings at the baths and on the beach.

In the Environs of Antioch

We were mystified in Antioch when we learned
of Julian's latest doings.

Apollo had made it clear to him at Daphne!
He would permit no oracle to be uttered (ah, what a shame!),
he had no intention of opening his prophetic mouth
until the sanctuary at Daphne was made pure.
The neighbouring dead, he declared, were distracting him.

There were many graves at Daphne.
And one of those buried there
was the holy and triumphant martyr, Babylas,
the splendour and glory of our church.

It was him the false god was hinting at, him he feared.
So long as Apollo felt him nearby, he didn't dare
publish his oracles; no, not a whisper came
(the false gods are terrified by our martyrs).

Impious Julian rolled up his sleeves,
lost control of himself and shouted: 'Dig deeper,
move him, take this Babylas away immediately.
Do you hear me over there? Apollo is angry.
Lift him out, take him away at once.
Exhume the body; put him wherever you want.
Just get him out, remove him. This is no game!
Apollo demanded we make his sanctuary pure.'

So we took him and bore the sacred relic away;
we took him, handling him with love and reverence.

And in fact, the sanctuary soon profited
from our labours. For it didn't take long at all
before a huge, terrifying fire started
and the entire precinct burned, along with Apollo.

The idol was burned to ash; destined for the rubbish-heap.

Julian exploded and spread the rumour –
what else could he do? – that the fire was started
by us Christians. Let him go on with his talk.
It was never proven: let him go on.
The important thing is, he exploded.

Notes

In the notes that follow I have tried to navigate a middle way between providing, on the one hand, a basic glossary of unfamiliar terms and, on the other, a full explication of the poems themselves. Where I thought it useful, I have included the date of a poem's composition or publication. More important, to my mind at least, is the source material that may have prompted a particular idea and a work's historical and mythological setting to provide context. Therefore I have included a number of passages from Homer, Plutarch and Gibbon, as well as some historical background where relevant. Quotations from the *Iliad* are drawn from the translation by Richmond Lattimore, *The Iliad of Homer* (University of Chicago Press, Chicago, 1951). Those from Plutarch's *Lives* are from the version by John Dryden (1683).

PART I: POEMS 1897–1904

Voices

Written on 12 July 1894, with the title 'Sweet Voices'; first published, in 1894, under that title. Rewritten in 1903 with the title 'Voices' and published in this form in 1904.

An Old Man

Written in 1894; published in 1897 with the heading *'Eheu Fugaces'* ('The Fleeting Years'), taken from Horace, *Odes* 11.14.

The First Step

Written in 1895 with the title 'The Last Step'; published in 1899 with the title 'The First Step'. The scene and the character of the young poet Eumenes are imagined. Theocritus (*fl.* 250 BC), the father of Greek pastoral poetry, was born in Syracuse in Sicily, and lived in Hellenistic Alexandria.

Interruption

This poem centres on two instances where the intervention by human parents foiled attempts by the gods to endow their mortal children with immortality. Demeter visited Eleusis in mourning after the abduction of her daughter Persephone by Hades. During her stay in the palace at Eleusis, Demeter attempted to make Demophoon, the queen Metaneira's son, immortal by placing him in an 'undying flame' (cf. *Homeric Hymn to Demeter*). Likewise, according to one version of the myth, Achilles was placed in fire at night by his mother, the river-goddess Thetis, in order to render him invulnerable, before the intervention of his father Peleus, king of Phthia in Thessaly. (See Apollonius, *Argonautica* IV.865–79, and Apollodorus, *History of the Gods* III.13.)

Thermopylae

Referring to Herodotus, *Histories* VII.176–223. Thermopylae was a narrow, fifty-foot-wide pass in Thessaly situated between Mount Oeta and the Aegean Sea. This slender corridor on the eastern side of mainland Greece is where the Greeks in 480 BC decided to make a stand against the invading Persians (the Medes). The Persian army, which according to Herodotus numbered in the hundreds of thousands, was on its way to Athens when it was held up at Thermopylae by a much smaller force, led by the Spartan commander Leonidas. On the evening of the second day of battle, Ephialtes, a Greek who lived in the area, revealed to the Persians a secret mountain path that led to the rear of the Greek forces defending the pass. Most of the Greek contingent, when they learned of the betrayal, retreated to Athens. But Leonidas and about three hundred of his troops stayed and fought to the death. The Persians would later get through and continue on their way to Athens, where they were defeated in the naval battle of Salamis.

Che Fece . . . Il Gran Rifiuto

The title is taken from Dante's *Inferno* III.59–60 ('*vidi e conobbi l'ombra di colui / che fece per viltà il gran rifiuto*' – 'I saw and knew the shade of him who through cowardice made the great refusal'). The passage is thought to refer to Celestine V, who was elected pope in 1294 but who went on to abdicate five months later at the insistence (according to some reports) of his successor Boniface VIII. Celestine V is omitted from the official list of popes. Dante sees the individual among a troop of 'neutral souls' who lived 'without disgrace and without praise', and whose common offence is *viltà*, or pusillanimity, the cowardice and meanness of nature by which a man refuses his calling.

Waiting for the Barbarians

The scene and dialogue are imagined. Cavafy in a note explains that because he chose the 'barbarians' as a symbol, it was natural for him to refer in the poem to emperors and senators, all reminiscent of a Roman scene. However, as he says, 'emperors, senators and orators are not exclusively Roman matters' (quoted from the Greek edition of Cavafy's verse, *Poems 1896–1933*, prepared by George Savidis (Ikaros, Athens, 1991), p. 174).

Lies

The epigraph seems to have been prompted by Plato's examination of poetry in his *Republic* and his decision to banish from his ideal state poets such as Homer and Aeschylus, who were deemed to have told 'lies' in their work.

The Funeral of Sarpedon

Written probably in 1892; published in 1898 under the title 'Ancient Days'. Based upon a passage from Homer's *Iliad*, book 16, ll. 663–83 (ll.663–75 quoted below). Sarpedon, lord of the Lycians, was Zeus' son through Laodameia (book 2, l. 876; book 6, ll.198–9). In book 15 (ll. 65–75) Zeus finally consents to Sarpedon's death at Patroclus' hand, in an act that will perpetuate the cycle of violence where Achilles kills Hector, and Apollo destroys Achilles.

> But the Achaians took from Sarpedon's shoulders the armour
> glaring and brazen, and this the warlike son of Menoitios
> gave to his companions to carry back to the hollow ships.
> And now Zeus who gathers the clouds spoke a word to Apollo:
> 'Go if you will, beloved Phoibos, and rescue Sarpedon
> from under the weapons, wash the dark suffusion of blood from him,
> then carry him far away and wash him in a running river,
> anoint him in ambrosia, put ambrosial clothing upon him;
> then give him into the charge of swift messengers to carry him,
> of Sleep and Death, who are twin brothers, and these two shall lay him
> down presently within the rich countryside of broad Lykia
> where his brothers and countrymen shall give him due burial
> with tomb and gravestone . . .'

The Horses of Achilles

Written in 1896; published in December 1897 under the title 'Ancient Days'. The horses of Achilles, Xanthus and Balius, were immortal. The poem is based upon a passage from Homer's *Iliad*, book 17, ll. 434–40:

> ... still as stands a grave monument which is set over
> the mounded tomb of a dead man or lady, they stood there
> holding motionless in its place the fair-wrought chariot,
> leaning their heads along the ground, and warm tears were running
> earthward from underneath the lids of the mourning horses
> who longed for their charioteer, while their bright manes were made dirty
> as they streamed down either side of the yoke from under the yoke pad.

PART II: POEMS 1905–1915

The Satrapy

A satrapy was a province governed by a provincial governor, or satrap, under the ancient Persian monarchy. Artaxerxes became king of Persia after the death of his father Xerxes in 464 BC. Artaxerxes' grandfather, Darius, had reorganized the empire and created satrapies, territorial units that also served as tax districts. He also founded Persepolis, where many administrative texts were discovered, and built a palace in Susa. This poem may have been influenced by Cavafy's reading about the last years of Themistocles' life in Plutarch, one of his favourite authors (*Themistocles* XXV). At around the end of the 470s, Themistocles, one of the greatest generals and political leaders of Greece's Golden Age, was ostracized from Athens, and after spending some time in the Peloponnese he proceeded to Asia Minor. The Athenians condemned him to death *in absentia*, and after 465 the new Persian king, Artaxerxes I, made him governor of Magnesia on the Meander river. However, Cavafy explains: 'The poet does not necessarily have in mind Themistocles or Demaratus, or any political person. The character implied is entirely symbolical, whom we should understand rather as an artist or scholar' (see Savidis, op. cit., p. 127). The word 'sophist', from the Greek *sophia* or 'wisdom', originally meant 'educator'. It acquired a more pejorative connotation in the second half of the fifth century BC, when 'sophists' came to mean a class of itinerant intellectuals and tutors who employed rhetoric to achieve their purposes, generally to persuade or convince others.

The Wise Perceive Imminent Events

First written in 1896 with the title 'Imminent Things'; published under the current title in 1899. Final version published in 1915. Apollonius of Tyana was, like Julian the Apostate, the source or inspiration for a number of Cavafy's poems. Philostratus' *Life of Apollonius* was described by Cavafy as a work 'full of poetic material', and at least four of the canonical poems include some reference to (or seem entirely prompted by) his reading of that author. The epigraph to this poem is taken from a passage describing the special capacities of this sage or prophet (*Life of Apollonius of Tyana* VIII.7). For more information on Apollonius of Tyana and Philostratus, see the note on 'If Indeed Dead' below.

The Ides of March

An imagined scene in a specific historical context. This poem was inspired by Cavafy's reading of Plutarch (*Life of Caesar* LXV), where the Greek philosopher Artemidorus is described as attempting to warn Caesar of the plot to kill him, on the morning of the Ides, 15 March 44 BC. (See also Shakespeare, *Julius Caesar* III.i.)

The God Abandoning Antony

The 'god' in question is Antony's patron deity, Dionysus (or Roman Bacchus), the god of drink and excess, on the night before Antony's showdown with Octavian outside Alexandria. The scene is lifted from Plutarch's *Life of Antony* LXXV:

> At supper, it is said, he bade his servants help him freely, and pour him out wine plentifully, since tomorrow, perhaps, they should not do the same, but be servants to a new master, whilst he should lie on the ground, a dead corpse, and nothing. His friends that were about him wept to hear him talk so; which he perceiving, told them he would not lead them to a battle in which he expected rather an honourable death than either safety or victory. That night, it is related, about the middle of it, when the whole city was in a deep silence and general sadness, expecting the event of the next day, on a sudden was heard the sound of all sorts of instruments and voices singing in tune, and the cry of a crowd of people shouting and dancing, like a troop of bacchants on its way ... People who reflected considered this to signify that Bacchus, the god whom Antony had always made it his study to copy and imitate, had now forsaken him.

In Shakespeare's *Antony and Cleopatra* IV.iii, Bacchus is transformed into Hercules: ''Tis the god Hercules, whom Antony loved, / Now leaves him.' Cavafy, in turn, transforms the god into the actual city of Alexandria, which takes its leave of Antony.

Theodotus

Theodotus of Chios was a schoolmaster hired to teach rhetoric to the young Egyptian king Ptolemy XIII. After Pompey's defeat in Pharsalus at the hands of Julius Caesar, Pompey cast about for a refuge and decided on Egypt, where he expected a favourable reception due to the treatment Pompey had earlier shown to the young Ptolemy's father. Theodotus, however, persuaded Ptolemy to kill Pompey when he landed, on 28 September, in 48 BC. The poem is drawn from Plutarch's *Life of Pompey*:

> Ptolemy himself was quite young, and therefore Pothinus, who had the principal administration of affairs, called a council of the chief men ... and commanded them every man to deliver his opinion touching the reception of Pompey. It was, indeed, a miserable thing that the fate of the great Pompey should be left to the determinations of Pothinus the eunuch, Theodotus of Chios, the paid rhetoric master, and Achillas, the Egyptian ... It seems they were so far different in their opinions that some were for sending the man away, and others, again, for inviting and receiving him; but Theodotus, to show his cleverness and the cogency of his rhetoric, undertook to demonstrate that neither the one nor the other was safe in that juncture of affairs.

Monotony

Written in 1898 with the title 'Like the Past'; published in 1908 under the current title.

Ithaca

The Cyclops and Laestrygonians were mythical monsters encountered by Odysseus during his ten-year voyage from Troy back to his home in Ithaca.

As Much As You Can

Written in 1905 with the title 'Life'; published in 1913 under the current title.

Trojans

Priam and Hecuba were the king and queen of Troy in Homer's *Iliad*.

King Demetrius

Demetrius Poliorcetes ('Besieger of Cities', 337–283 BC), the son of Antigonus I. He fought as his father's lieutenant throughout the Hellenistic Mediterranean, at the liberation of Athens from the regime of Demetrius of Phaleron in 307 and in a year-long siege of Rhodes (305–304 BC) in which he earned his notorious sobriquet. He was proclaimed king of Macedonia in 294 following his assassination of Alexander V, and held the throne for six and a half years. His objective as king was the reconquest of his father's empire, and in 288 he prepared a fleet of 500 ships to achieve this Alexander-like ambition. However, Plutarch describes him as a mere impersonation of Alexander the Great, like an actor on a stage: 'And Demetrius truly was a perfect play and pageant, with his robes and diadems, his gold-edged purple and his hats with double streamers, his very shoes being of the richest purple felt, embroidered over in gold.' Hearing the news of Demetrius' massive build-up in arms, Seleucus, Lysimachus, Ptolemy I and Pyrrhus allied against him and, facing such a combined force, Demetrius' army chose to abandon the field in a group mutiny. The last lines are lifted more or less directly from Plutarch's *Life of Demetrius* XLIV.

The Glory of the Ptolemies

The poem is a dramatic monologue in the person of one of the Lagids, the name given to members of the Ptolemaic dynasty that ruled Egypt from 323 to 30 BC. While it is not clear which of the Lagid kings Cavafy specifically had in mind, it may have been Ptolemy II Philadelphus (285–246 BC), who made Alexandria a centre of the arts and learning. The Seleucid Empire was one of the three successor states (along with the Ptolemaic and Macedonian regimes) to Alexander the Great's conquests in the East. It ranged from Central Anatolia all the way to the Indus Valley. The name derives from one of Alexander's generals, Seleucus, who was the first in a dynasty that lasted almost three hundred years, with over thirty kings. The dynasty of the Ptolemies, or Lagids, was its sibling state, named likewise for the general under Alexander (Lagus) who took control of that portion of Alexander's domains.

The Procession of Dionysus

Damon is very likely an imaginary character, but the Syracusan king referred to is probably Hieron II, who reigned from about 270 BC. The characters translated as Licence, Intoxication, Sweetwine, Melody, Tunesweet, Revelry and Ceremony were the personifications of the demigods who attended upon Dionysus (or Roman Bacchus) at his festivals. Parian marble denotes the fine-grained, supremely white marble from the island of Paros in the Cyclades, which was highly prized by Greek sculptors and their patrons. Some of the greatest extant masterpieces of Greek sculpture are in this type of marble.

The Battle of Magnesia

A complex historical poem, shifting swiftly from first-person commands to third-person narrative. The subject is Philip V (238–179 BC), king of Macedonia, who was defeated by the Romans in 197 BC at Cynoscephalae, and was then confined by the Romans to Macedonia. The poem is an imagined description of Philip's reactions to the defeat of Antiochus the Great, seven years later, in the battle of Magnesia (in 190 BC), which marked the end of any further Greek opposition to Roman hegemony in the Mediterranean.

The Displeasure of the Seleucid

The Seleucid Demetrius (187–150 BC), the future Demetrius I Soter, king of Syria, was held as a hostage in Rome for sixteen years, until 162 BC (see the note on 'Of Demetrius, Soter (162–150 BC)' below). The Ptolemy of this poem, Ptolemy VI Philometor (180–145 BC), was dethroned by his brother Ptolemy VIII Euergetes, or Benefactor, in 164, and went to Rome in that year to ask for the Roman Senate's aid in restoring him to power. (See also the note on 'Envoys from Alexandria' below.) The scene is described in Diodorus Siculus, *Historical Library* XXXI. See the note on 'The Glory of the Ptolemies' above for more information on the Seleucid and Lagid dynasties.

Orophernes

Orophernes was the bastard son of the king of Cappadocia, Ariarathus IV (called Eusebis, or the Pious, 220–163 BC). In 157 BC Orophernes usurped the throne of his brother, Ariarathus V, with the support of the king of Syria, Demetrius I Soter. But his reign was so dissolute that he was thrown out by his own subjects before a year was up. Orophernes then tried and failed to take Demetrius Soter's throne, and later died in 154 BC. His story is told in Polybius,

The Histories XXXII, and Athenaeus, *Deipnosophists* X. The tetradrachmon, literally 'four drachmas', was the most widely distributed coin in fifth-century Greece up to the rule of Alexander the Great.

Alexandrian Kings

The poem describes the celebration organized by Antony in 34 BC and held in the grandiose and newly built Gymnasium of Alexandria. In the ceremony, Antony was symbolically carving up the kingdom of Alexander the Great in order to bestow it upon his and Julius Caesar's heirs. Alexander and Ptolemy were Antony's sons; Caesarion was the son of Julius Caesar. In the ceremony Cleopatra VII (69–30 BC) was named Queen of Kings, and Caesarion, who was thirteen years of age at the time, was named King of Kings. Four years later, Antony and Cleopatra would commit suicide, Caesarion would later be executed, and the other children taken as hostages to Rome. See Plutarch's *Life of Antony* LIV:

> It seemed a theatrical piece of insolence and contempt for his country. For assembling the people in the exercise ground, and causing two golden thrones to be placed on a platform of silver, the one for him and the other for Cleopatra, and at their feet lower thrones for their children, he [Antony] proclaimed Cleopatra Queen of Egypt, Cyprus, Libya and Coele-Syria, and with her conjointly Caesarion, the reputed son of the former Caesar, who left Cleopatra with child. His own sons by Cleopatra were to have the style of king of kings; to Alexander he gave Armenia and Media, with Parthia, so soon as it should be overcome; to Ptolemy, Phoenicia, Syria and Cilicia. Alexander was brought out before the people in Median costume, the tiara and upright peak, and Ptolemy in boots and mantle and Macedonian cap done about with the diadem.

Philhellene

Written in 1906; published in 1912. A fictional historical poem in the voice of an administrator or kinglet of the satrapy of Phraata in eastern Iran instructing his assistant or courtier Sithaspes on how to manage the appearance of his coinage. Zagros is a mountain range in the area of modern-day Iraq. For a note on the sophists, and more on 'satrapy', see 'The Satrapy' above.

The Footsteps

Written in 1893 under the title 'The Footsteps of the Eumenides'; rewritten with its current title in 1908 and published in 1909. The poem describes a moment in the life of Nero (originally named Lucius Domitius Ahenobarbus, AD 37–68). In AD 59, Nero had his mother Agrippina killed because she disapproved of his affair with Poppaea Sabina. Lares are miniature roman 'gods of the household' that maintain the ancestral spirits of the family. The furies (or Erinyes) are the chthonic deities of revenge and family trespass. They were most famously represented in Aeschylus' *Eumenides* as the avenging furies in pursuit of Orestes for the murder of his mother Clytaemnestra. Ahenobarbus is the gens name of Nero's family, which included a number of prominent Romans of the late republic and early principate.

Herodes Atticus

Claudius Atticus Herodes (AD 101–77), a famous sophist (see the note on 'The Satrapy' above) of the second century AD who divided his time between Rome (where he taught Marcus Aurelius, among others) and his luxurious home outside Athens, near the town of Marathon. His rival was Alexander of Seleucia (see Philostratus, *Lives of the Sophists* v.571).

Tyanian Sculptor

First written in 1893 under the title 'Sculptor's Workshop'; rewritten in 1903 and published in 1911 with the current title. A historical dramatic monologue set in Rome involving an anonymous and imagined artist originally from Tyana in Cappadocia. The muster roll of heroic Roman busts (doubtless commissions from the senators mentioned in the poem) includes Marius (157–86 BC), Lucius Aemilius Paullus (d. 160 BC), Scipio Africanus Major (236–183 BC) and Minor (185–129 BC). (It is unclear which of the two, Scipio Major or Minor, Cavafy has in mind here.) Caesarion, otherwise known as Ptolemy XV, born in 47 BC, was the eldest son of Cleopatra VII and Julius Caesar. He was executed by Octavian (Augustus) in 30 BC. Rhea is the female offspring of Sky (Uranus) and Earth (Gaia) in Greek mythology. She was sister and wife to Cronus and mother of Zeus, Poseidon, Demeter and others. In Roman mythology, she was the equivalent of the Magna Mater, the Great Mother. In art, Rhea is usually depicted on a chariot drawn by two lions. Patroclus, the son of Menoetius, was Achilles' friend and lover at Troy.

The Tomb of the Grammarian Lysias

The hero of the poem is a fictional character.

The Tomb of Eurion

Written in 1912; published in 1914. Syenite is a coarse-grained rock of the same general composition as granite. Arsinoe was an ancient city on the coast of Cilicia in modern-day Turkey. The city was founded by Ptolemy Philadelphus and named for Arsinoe II of Egypt, his sister and wife. Aristocleitus and Paros were sophist-tutors of minor status.

That's the Man!

The fictional poet described in this poem comes from Edessa, capital of Osroene, a Roman protectorate but largely Semitic in its population. The reference to Lucian (a comic writer of Samosata in Syria, born c. AD 115) is from his work *The Dream, or Lucian's Career*. In Lucian's 'dream', the figure of 'Culture' explains to Lucian that he will become so famous a writer that even when he is abroad people will immediately take note of his genius and exclaim in admiration: 'That's the man!'

Dangerous Things

An imaginary scene and character. Myrtias is a Syrian student in Alexandria during the reign of Constantius II (AD 337–61). Constantius was the second and Constans the third of the three sons of Constantine I and his second wife, Fausta. When Constantine died in 337, Constantius, his older brother Constantine II, and his younger brother Constans divided the Roman Empire among them. Constantine II received Britannia, Gaul and Hispania; Constans ruled Italy, Africa and Illyricum; and Constantius ruled the East. This division changed when Constantine II died in 340, trying to overthrow Constans in Italy, and Constans became sole ruler in the western half of the empire.

Manuel Comnenus

Byzantine emperor from 1143 to 1180, Manuel Comnenus dreamed of a reconstituted Roman Empire, and transformed the austere court of his father, John Comnenus, into a sumptuous realm of ceremony and magnificence. He expended much of his kingdom's resources in campaigns largely targeting his western neighbours and the Crusader states, which distracted him from the growing threat in the east from the Seljuq Turks. He was defeated by the Turks at Myriocephalon in 1176. (See Nicetas, *Histories* VII.)

Ionic

Although there is no direct historical reference in this poem, some think it is meant to occur somewhere between the eighth to ninth centuries AD when iconoclasm – literally a 'breaking of the icons', the deliberate destruction of a culture's religious symbols or monuments – was perhaps most pronounced, and many of the pagan temples in Asia Minor were destroyed by iconoclast Christians. The iconoclast edict was promulgated by Leo III in 730. Ionia is an ancient region of western Asia Minor along the coast of the Aegean Sea. Greek settlers established colonies here before 1000 BC.

PART III: POEMS 1916–1918

Before the Statue of Endymion

Endymion was a mythic shepherd boy, the beloved of Selene or the Moon. Selene begged Zeus to grant Endymion eternal life so that she might be able to embrace him forever. Zeus complained, but put Endymion into eternal sleep. Each night thereafter, Selene visited him on Mount Latmus, near Miletus, in Asia Minor.

Envoys from Alexandria

A scene invented by Cavafy depicting the rival kings Ptolemy VI Philometor and his brother Ptolemy VIII Euergetes, who together ruled Egypt jointly from 170 to 164 BC. In 164, when Euergetes refused to continue the joint reign, ousting his brother from the throne, Philometor went to Rome to ask for the Senate's help in restoring him to power, which came to pass in the following year. For a note on the Lagids, see 'The Glory of the Ptolemies' above.

Aristobulus

Aristobulus was the last scion of the Hasmonean royal house (see below). He was a favourite of the people on account of his noble descent and handsome presence, and thus became an object of fear to Herod (73–4 BC), who at first sought to ignore him entirely by debarring him from the high priesthood. But his mother Alexandra compelled Herod to appoint him to the office of high priest. As Herod dared not resort to open violence, he caused him to be drowned (35 BC) while he was bathing in Jericho. Cyprus was Herod's mother, Miriam – Aristobulus' sister – was his wife and Salome was his sister. (See Josephus, *The Jewish War and Antiquities*.) The Hasmoneans were the ruling dynasty of the Hasmonean kingdom (140–37 BC), an autonomous Jewish state in ancient Israel. The Hasmonean dynasty was established under the leadership of Simon Maccabeus, two decades after his brother Judas defeated the Seleucid army in 165 BC. (For more information, see the note on 'Alexander Jannaeus and Alexandra' below.) 'Ephebe' is the Greek term for a youth, often one in training, and usually of an age before the beard's first growth.

Caesarion

Caesarion was the son of Cleopatra by Julius Caesar. Mark Antony made him king of Egypt in 34 BC (see the note on 'Alexandrian Kings' above), but in 30 BC he was executed by Octavian, the adopted son of Julius Caesar. Octavian ordered the execution after consulting Arrius, an Alexandrian philosopher, who justified the murder by reference to the quote from Homer's *Iliad* (book 2, l. 204) that 'too many kings are not well'. (See Plutarch, *Life of Antony* LIV.) Berenice was the name of a series of Egyptian (and Judean) princesses or other members of the Ptolemaic dynasty in Egypt.

Nero's Deadline

Nero Claudius Caesar (AD 37–68) was emperor of Rome from 54 to 68. In AD 67, Nero journeyed to Greece to explore and enjoy Greek culture, visiting the Delphic oracle on this trip. In 68, the Roman army petitioned Galba, Spain's governor, to take up the imperial throne. Nero returned to Rome in 68 where the Senate declared him a public enemy. He committed suicide after Galba accepted the army's proposition. The oracle's prophecy and its double meaning are also described by Suetonius in the *Life of Nero* XL.

The Tomb of Lanes

Hyacinth was a beautiful youth beloved by the god Apollo. According to myth, the two competed at discus, taking turns throwing it, until Apollo, to impress his beloved, threw it with all his might. Hyacinth ran to catch it, to impress Apollo in turn, and was struck by the discus as it fell to the ground, and died. Apollo did not allow Hades to claim the boy; rather, he made a flower, the hyacinth, from his spilled blood.

The Tomb of Iases

Narcissus, in myth, was a boy renowned for his beauty but preoccupied with his own image. In Ovid's *Metamorphoses* (book III), the proud and unfeeling Narcissus is punished by the gods for having spurned all his male suitors.

In a Town of Osroene

The kingdom of Osroene was in northwestern Mesopotamia. *Charmides* is the title of a Platonic dialogue exploring the question of temperance. In the dialogue, Socrates is described as becoming aroused at the sight of the noble youth Charmides on a visit to the Athenian palaestra or wrestling grounds:

> I asked whether any of them were remarkable for wisdom or beauty, or both ... when I saw him [Charmides] coming in, I confess that I was quite astonished at his beauty and stature; all the world seemed to be enamoured of him; amazement and confusion reigned when he entered; and a troop of lovers followed him ... And at that moment all the people in the palaestra crowded about us, and, O rare! I caught a sight of the inwards of his garment, and took the flame. Then I could no longer contain myself.
>
> From Plato's *Charmides*, translated by Benjamin Jowett

In the Month of Athyr

Athyr is November in the Egyptian calendar. The Greek letters Kappa and Zeta form the number 27 in Greek.

For Ammones, Who Died at Twenty-nine, in the Year 610

The characters in this poem appear to be entirely fictional.

Aemilianus Monai, Alexandrian, AD 628–655

Like so many of Cavafy's tombstone inscriptions, this one too is imaginary. The scene is Byzantine Sicily of the seventh century.

PART IV: POEMS 1919–1933

Of the Jews, AD 50

Ianthes is a Greek name and Antony Roman, suggesting that this was already a clearly 'Hellenizing' or assimilated Jewish family of Alexandria. For a note on Endymion, see 'Before the Statue of Endymion' above.

Imenos

Michael the Third was the emperor of Byzantium from 842 to 867, the last prince of the Phrygian dynasty. His epithet was the 'Drunkard'. Cavafy places the imaginary Imenos in Sicily during the last years of the Byzantine occupation of that island.

Of Demetrius Soter (162–150 BC)

Demetrius Soter (the 'Saviour') was the son of King Seleucus Philopater, or Seleucus IV, and grandson of Antiochus III the Great. He was brought up in Rome as a hostage. In 162 BC, at the age of twenty-five, he escaped with the help of the Greek historian Polybius and regained the throne of Syria (by assassinating his cousin Antiochus V). There he expelled the satrap of Babylon, Timarchus (brother of Heracleides – see the note on 'Craftsman of Wine Bowls' below), and tried to re-establish the unity and hegemony of the Syrian dynasty, but was afterwards defeated by the adventurer Alexander Balas (150 BC). (See Polybius, *The Histories* XXXI, and Diodorus Siculus, *Historical Library* XXXI.) For a note on the battle of Magnesia, see 'The Battle of Magnesia' above.

If Indeed Dead

Apollonius of Tyana (born in 4 BC) was a Greek Pythagorean philosopher and sage who was venerated by his disciples as a sort of Christ figure. He enjoyed wide fame for his teachings, his ascetic example, and the many miracles he worked. An account of his life was written by the itinerant professor and historian Philostratus (AD 172–249), in a work that enjoyed great popularity during the period when paganism was in decline. The biography is based in part on the memoirs of an Assyrian disciple of Apollonius named Damis. Justin the Elder is Justin I, Byzantine emperor from AD 518 to 527. The title is a quotation from Philostratus' *Life of Apollonius of Tyana* VIII.

Young Men of Sidon (AD 400)

Sidon was a Hellenized city in Phoenicia. The poets mentioned are all well represented in the ancient collection of elegiac and epigrammatic poetry known as the *Palatine Anthology*. Meleager was from Syria. Crinagoras was from Mytilene on Lesbos. Rhianus was a poet from Crete. All wrote erotic or epigrammatic poetry of only a few lines in length. Aeschylus is the first of the great Athenian tragedians. He was born in 525 BC in Eleusis, near Athens, and died in Sicily in 456. Aeschylus took part in the battle of Marathon in 490 BC and lost his brother during the fighting. Datis and Ataphernes were Persian commanders at the battle. The epitaph on Aeschylus is genuine; however, it is doubtful that it was written by the playwright himself. The three works mentioned towards the end of the poem are all tragedies by him.

Darius

The episode depicted here takes place at Amisos in Asia Minor around 74 BC, during the reign of Mithridates VI Eupator. Mithridates was the Persian king of Pontus from 120 to 63 BC who claimed descent from the Achaemenid dynasty. The Achaemenid or Persian Empire was founded by Cyrus the Great, who became king of Persia in 559 BC. Darius, the great Achaemenid king (521–486 BC), was ruler of Persia when the battle of Marathon took place in 490. After Alexander's death in Babylon (11 June 323), his empire was divided into three parts: Macedonia was ruled by Antipater, Ptolemy reconstituted the Egyptian kingdom, and Seleucus ruled the Asian parts of Alexander's realms – in fact, the Seleucid Empire was a continuation of the Achaemenid Empire. The fictional poet Phernazes is hoping to dedicate his epic poem *Darius* to King Mithridates. The Romans conquered Amisos in 71 BC.

Anna Comnena

Born in 1083, Anna Comnena was the first daughter of Alexius I Comnenus, emperor of Byzantium from 1081 to 1118. After her father died, Anna attempted to depose her younger brother, John, who was Alexius' true heir, in favour of her own husband, Nicephorus Bryennius. The quotes are from Anna's epic poem *The Alexiad*, written after her husband's death when she withdrew to a convent. (See Nicetas, *Histories* I.)

Byzantine Aristocrat, in Exile, Composing Verses

Nicephorus III Botaniates became emperor of Byzantium in 1078, having ousted Michael VII. In 1081, Botaniates was supplanted by Alexius I Comnenus, husband of Irene Ducas.

The Favourite of Alexander Balas

Alexander Balas, the pretender son of Antiochus IV Epiphanes (king of Syria from 175 to 164 BC), took the throne of Syria from Demetrius I Soter in 150 BC with the assent of Rome and the armed assistance of Ptolemy Philometor of Egypt. Balas was born in Smyrna and came from an impoverished family. An adventurer, without any political skills, he was assassinated in 145.

The Melancholy of Jason Cleander, Poet in
Commagene, AD 595

Cleander is an invented character. Commagene was on the Euphrates river and was in turn Assyrian, Seleucid, Byzantine and then Arab. At the end of the sixth century AD the area was still under Byzantine control; in 638 it fell to the Arabs. (See also the note on 'Epitaph of Antiochus, King of Commagene' below.)

Demaratus

Demaratus was joint king of Sparta, together with Cleomenes, from 515 to 491 BC. In 491, in collusion with Leotychides, and with the help of a bribed Delphic oracle, Cleomenes had Demaratus deposed on the grounds that he was not the legitimate heir to the throne, and Cleomenes became joint king with Leotychides. Demaratus sought refuge with Darius, the king of Persia, and accompanied Xerxes on his invasion of Greece. He is mentioned in Herodotus' *Histories*, books VI and VII. Porphyry (AD 234–305) was a teacher of rhetoric in Rome and the writer of the sketch is probably one of his students. For a note on the sophists, see 'The Satrapy' above.

From the School of the Renowned Philosopher

The 'renowned philosopher' is Ammonius Saccas (d. 243). He was a Christian philosopher based in Alexandria, the so-called 'Socrates of Neoplatonism', and is thought also to have taught Origen, Plotinus and Longinus, among others. An 'eparchy' was originally the name of one of the divisions of the Roman Empire. Diocletian (AD 284–305) and Maximian divided the empire into four great prefectures (Gaul, Italy, Illyricum and the East). Each was subdivided into (civil) dioceses, and these again into eparchies under governors. The church accepted this division as a convenient one for later use. An eparch was simply the governor or, later, chief bishop of an eparchy.

Craftsman of Wine Bowls

The Romans defeated Antiochus III the Great (king of Syria 223–187 BC) at Magnesia in 190. Heracleides, the treasurer of Antiochus IV Epiphanes (215–164 BC), went to Rome at around 175 to lead an embassy on behalf of Antiochus Epiphanes to regain the Syrian throne. He was later banished by Demetrius I Soter, the successor of Antiochus in 162 (see the note on 'Of Demetrius Soter (162–150 BC)' above), and then supported the adventurer Alexander Balas (see the note on 'The Favourite of Alexander Balas' above). (See Polybius, *The Histories* XXXIII.)

For Those Who Fought in the Achaean League

The Achaean League was an alliance of the twelve cities of Achaea in the north-eastern Peloponnese in Greece. The Achaean War, fought in 146–145 BC, brought Rome and the Achaean League together in the league's final battle. Critolaus was the general of the 'league' and was defeated by the Romans, led by Q. Caecilius Metellus, in 146 BC. Diaeus succeeded Critolaus and was himself defeated near Corinth in the same year by L. Mummius Achaicus. Ptolemy VIII Lathyrus was king of Egypt 117–107 BC and again 89–81 BC.

To Antiochus Epiphanes

Antiochus IV Epiphanes (king of Syria 175–164 BC) was the son of Antiochus III the Great, whom the Romans had defeated at Magnesia in 190 BC. After his brother Seleucus IV Philopator (ruler of the Seleucid Empire 187–175 BC) was assassinated, Seleucus' daughter Laodice married Perseus, the last king of Macedonia. Perseus was defeated by the Roman general and politician Aemilius Paullus at Pydna in 168 BC, marking the end of Greek independence and the start of Roman hegemony in the East.

Julian, Seeing the Contempt

Julian the Apostate, emperor of Rome AD 361–3, attempted to reform and reintroduce paganism as the official Roman religion, organized on a foundation of Neoplatonic philosophical conceits. The quotation that opens the poem is taken from one of Julian's letters to Theodorus, appointing him high priest 'of all the temples in Asia'. Christianity had been made, in effect, the official religion of the empire by Constantine the Great in AD 324. In his satirical sketch *Misopogon* (see the note on 'Julian and the Antiochians' below), Julian attacked what he saw as Christian decadence in Antioch.

Epitaph of Antiochus, King of Commagene

Commagene was a district of Syria on the Euphrates river, and its capital was Samosata. It had several kings, a number of whom went by the name Antiochus, but the most famous of these was Antiochus I – the only child of King Mithridates I Callinicus and Queen Laodice VII Thea of Commagene – who ruled 70–38 BC. He was able to keep Commagene independent (by allying himself with Pompey in 64 BC) even as Rome consolidated its power in the East. He was half Parthian and half Greek by birth. For a note on the sophists, see 'The Satrapy' above.

Julian in Nicomedia

Before becoming emperor of Rome (AD 361–3), Julian was forced to veil his anti-Christian tendencies from the Christian majority. The emperor Constantius II, Julian's cousin, had ordered a strict Christian education for both Julian and his half-brother Gallus, who was later executed by Constantius in AD 354. Maximus of Ephesus was a Neoplatonic philosopher and miracle-worker. His chief title to fame is the influence, plainly mischievous, that he gained over the emperor Julian. Chrysanthius likewise was a sophist and theurge who was also within Julian's circle. All three were students of the Neoplatonic philosopher Aedesius. Mardonius was Julian's tutor, and a eunuch. Nicomedia, where Julian lived for a short period, was the capital of Bithynia in Asia Minor.

The Year 31 BC in Alexandria

The year 31 BC was when Antony, along with Cleopatra, was defeated by Octavian off the western coast of Greece at Actium. Antony committed suicide just before Octavian entered Alexandria the following year.

John Cantacuzenus Has the Upper Hand

An unnamed nobleman of the empire describes the consequences of his involvement in the civil war following the death of Andronicus III Palaeologus in 1341. The new Byzantine emperor, John V, was eleven years old when a power struggle arose between the widowed Empress Anna of Savoy and the regent John Cantacuzenus, who was crowned emperor as John VI in 1347. Irene, daughter of Andronicus Asan (see the note on 'Of Coloured Glass' below), was John Cantacuzenus' wife.

Temethus, Antiochian, AD 400

Antiochus IV Epiphanes reigned in Syria from 175 to 164 BC. There is no record of the friend identified as 'Emonides' in this poem and he is most likely fictional. Syrians referred to the dynasty of the Seleucids (see the note on 'The Glory of the Ptolemies' above) as the 'Kingdom of the Greeks'.

Of Coloured Glass

This poem was inspired by the ceremony in 1347 that combined the crowning of John Cantacuzenus (see the note on 'John Cantacuzenus Has the Upper Hand' above) as emperor with the wedding of his daughter Helen to John V Palaeologus, although the wedding is not referred to in the poem. Andronicus Asan, Cantacuzenus' father-in-law, was a son of Ivan Asen III of Bulgaria and Irene Palaiologina. Gibbon (*Decline and Fall* LXIII) describes the 'proud poverty' of the Byzantine throne during this period:

> The festival of the coronation and nuptials was celebrated with the appearances of concord and magnificence, and both were equally fallacious. During the late troubles, the treasures of the state, and even the furniture of the palace, had been alienated or embezzled; the royal banquet was served in pewter or earthenware; and such was the proud poverty of the times, that the absence of gold and jewels was supplied by the paltry artifices of glass and gilt-leather.

On Italy's Coast

Magna Graecia encompassed southern Italy and Sicily, an area that had been widely colonized by the Greeks from the seventh century BC onwards. The boy Kimos (a Greek name) is described as 'Italiotes', meaning an Italian of Greek descent; hence the division of loyalties described in the poem. The booty mentioned in the poem was from the sack of Corinth by the Romans in 146 BC by the Roman general L. Mummius Achaicus.

Apollonius of Tyana in Rhodes

This poem may have been inspired by an actual incident described in the *Life of Apollonius* by Philostratus (book v, ch. 22). The sage or 'prophet' was castigating a young Rhodian who had lavished a great deal of money on the building and décor of his house, but had spent relatively little on his own education. For more information on Apollonius of Tyana and Philostratus, see the note on 'If Indeed Dead' above.

In a Town of Asia Minor

The naval battle of Actium (31 BC) marked the end of Antony's success in the East and the beginning of the Roman Empire under Octavian, soon to be renamed Augustus.

Priest at the Serapeion

The famous temple of Serapis (the Serapeion), built by Ptolemy III (*fl.* 246–22 BC), was destroyed during the persecution of the pagans initiated by the Christian emperor Theodosius in AD 391.

A Great Procession of Clergy and Laymen

Just after his visit to Antioch in AD 362, Julian died fighting the Persians (AD 363) and Jovian was promptly elected emperor by the army. Jovian was a tolerant Christian, but reigned for a mere seven months. Gibbon (*Decline and Fall* xxv) provides a gloss on the feelings of the Christians, however short-lived, surrounding the pious successor of Julian:

> The Christians were unanimous in the loud and sincere applause which they bestowed on the pious successor of Julian ... Under his reign Christianity obtained an easy and lasting victory; and as soon as the smile of royal patronage was withdrawn, the genius of Paganism, which had been fondly raised and cherished by the arts of Julian, sunk irrecoverably in the dust. In many cities the temples were shut or deserted; the philosophers, who had abused their transient favour, thought it prudent to shave their beards and disguise their profession; and the Christians rejoiced that they were now in a condition to forgive or to revenge the injuries which they had suffered under the preceding reign.

Scholar Departing Syria

The stater was an ancient coin of Greek origin which circulated from about 700 to 50 BC; its value was the equivalent of a tetradrachmon (four drachmas).

Julian and the Antiochians

Julian wrote *Misopogon* ('The Beard Hater') as a satire directed against both his own interest in philosophy and against the Antiochians themselves. Constantius was his cousin and predecessor on the imperial throne (see the note on 'Julian in Nicomedia' above).

Anna Dalassena

Anna was the mother of Alexius Comnenus, whose reign endured from 1081 to 1118. The Golden Bull (the 'imperial decree' issued by Alexius to promote Venetian trade) appointed his mother Regent of the Empire, and is quoted in her granddaughter Anna Comnena's *Alexiad* III.6. For more information, see the note on 'Anna Comnena' above.

Greek Since Antiquity

Antioch was founded in 300 BC by Seleucus I and quickly became one of the capitals of the Seleucid Empire. The story of Io, the daughter of Inachus, king of Argos in the Peloponnese, is told in Aeschylus'

Prometheus Bound, as well as Ovid's *Metamorphoses* (book 1, 568 ff.). Zeus fell in love with Io but this aroused Hera's anger and so he changed Io into a heifer in order to hide her. Hera then sent a gadfly to torment Io, driving her on a seemingly haphazard odyssey across the ancient world, east to Egypt and the Caucasus mountains and finally to Syria, where she died. The tale of her wanderings is foretold by Prometheus in Aeschylus' play. Ione or Iopolis (the 'city of Io') was built by her Argive brothers on the site where she finally died. Iopolis was renamed Antioch by Seleucus when he founded the new city in 300 BC. The Antiochians continued to commemorate the connection with ancient Argos through festivals and ceremonies. Gibbon (*Decline and Fall* XXIV) describes Antioch and its inhabitants as follows:

> The warmth of the climate disposed the natives to the most intemperate enjoyment of tranquillity and opulence, and the lively licentiousness of the Greeks was blended with the hereditary softness of the Syrians. Fashion was the only law, pleasure the only pursuit, and the splendour of dress and furniture was the only distinction of the citizens of Antioch. The arts of luxury were honoured, the serious and manly virtues were the subject of ridicule, and the contempt for female modesty and reverent age announced the universal corruption of the capital of the East. The love of spectacles was the taste, or rather passion, of the Syrians; the most skilful artists were procured from the adjacent cities; a considerable share of the revenue was devoted to the public amusements, and the magnificence of the games of the theatre and circus was considered as the happiness and as the glory of Antioch.

You Did Not Understand

The quote referred to in the poem is taken from a letter that Julian wrote to Basil of Caesarea (AD 330–79), one of the Fathers of the Christian church. Basil is known, among other things, for having penned a letter of his own that attempted to explain how Classical literature should be interpreted and used in the education of Christians. Julian's letter is quoted in the *Ecclesiastical History* (V.18) written by the fifth-century author Sozomen, who suggests that the purpose of Julian's letter was to show his contempt for the bishops' Christianized versions of the ancient Classics. The answer of the bishops, quoted in the poem, is also drawn from Sozomen's text.

In Sparta

Cleomenes was king of Sparta from 236 to 222 BC. The Ptolemy referred to in the poem is Ptolemy III Euergetes, king of Egypt at the time, who promised to assist Cleomenes in his war against Macedonia and the Achaean League (see the note on 'For Those Who Fought in the Achaean League' above) on condition that he send his mother (Cratesiclea) and children to Egypt as hostages. The Ptolemies were descended from the Lagid family (see the note on 'The Glory of the Ptolemies' above), a clan of rather low Macedonian birth, and so from the perspective of the more ancient genealogy of the Spartans, their dynasty was much younger and less esteemed. See Plutarch, *Life of Agis and Cleomenes* XXXVII:

> Now Ptolemy, the king of Egypt, promised him assistance, but demanded his mother and children for hostages. This, for some considerable time, he was ashamed to discover to his mother; and though he often went to her on purpose, and was just upon the discourse, yet he still refrained, and kept it to himself; so that she began to suspect, and asked his friends, whether Cleomenes had something to say to her, which he was afraid to speak. At last, Cleomenes venturing to tell her, she laughed aloud, and said, 'Was this the thing that you had so often a mind to tell me, and were afraid? Make haste and put me on ship-board, and send this carcass where it may be most serviceable to Sparta, before age destroys it unprofitably here.'

A Prince from Western Libya

Aristomenes and Menelaus are invented characters.

Cimon, Son of Learchos, Twenty-two Years of Age, Student of Greek Literature (in Cyrene)

Cyrene was a major Greek colony in North Africa, an important centre of trade and literature. Callimachus (305–240 BC), one of the most important Hellenistic poets, was born there, as were the philosophers Aristippus and Carneades.

On the March to Sinope

Mithridates V Euergetes, king of Pontus from 156 to 120 BC, is the Mithridates described in this poem. He was assassinated by conspirators within his own court at Sinope. Mithridates' encounter with the seer en route to Sinope seems to have been invented by Cavafy. The 'ancestor's companion' referred to in the poem was Demetrius (337–283 BC), king of Macedonia (see the note on 'King Demetrius' above), who had saved the life of Mithridates II (337–302 BC) during his stay at the court of Demetrius' father, Antigonus. In a dream Antigonus was prompted to kill the young guest, but when

Demetrius heard of this plan he warned Mithridates, scratching in the ground with the end of his spear the words: 'Run, Mithridates.' (See Plutarch, *Life of Demetrius*.)

Myres: Alexandria, AD 340

For a note on the term 'Serapeion', see 'Priest at the Serapeion' above.

Alexander Jannaeus and Alexandra

Alexander Jannaeus, son of Joannes Hyrcanus and brother of Aristobulus I (whose widow Alexandra, also known as Salome, he married), reigned as king of the Jews at Jerusalem from 103 to 76 BC. The revolt of the Jews against Antiochus IV Epiphanes led by the house of the Hasmoneans, with Judas Maccabeus and his brothers (John, Jonathan, Simon and Eleazar) at their head, consisted of a long series of battles, which in the end gave the Jews their independence for about a century. That independence, however, was as relative as it was short-lived, and Hasmonean power over Judea passed once again to the Romans soon after Alexander's successor died in 67 BC. The coins of Alexander's reign bore Greek as well as Hebrew and Aramaic inscriptions. For a note on the Seleucids, see 'The Glory of the Ptolemies' above.

Come, O King of the Lacedaemonians

The scene described by Cavafy in this poem is inspired by Plutarch's *Life of Agis and Cleomenes* XXXVII (quoted below). Cratesiclea was executed soon after her son's protector, Ptolemy III, died, in the reign of Ptolemy IV. For more information, see the note on 'In Sparta' above.

> Therefore, all things being provided for the voyage, they went by land to Taenarus, and the army waited on them. Cratesiclea, when she was ready to go on board, took Cleomenes aside into Neptune's temple and embracing him, who was much dejected and extremely discomposed, she said, 'Go to, King of Sparta; when we come forth at the door, let none see us weep, or show any passion that is unworthy of Sparta, for that alone is in our own power; as for success or disappointment, those wait on us as the deity decrees.'

They Should Have Taken the Time

The poem's dramatic context can be dated to sometime between 133 and 125 BC. The name Malefactor ('Kakergetes') is a sarcastic reference to Ptolemy VIII Euergetes ('Benefactor'), ruler of Egypt from

145 to 116 BC, also known as 'Physcon', or 'Bladder'. (See also the note on 'Envoys from Alexandria' above.) Zabinas was a pretender to the throne of Syria who with the help of Physcon assumed the throne there in 128 BC by defeating Demetrius II Nicator. Zabinas was later defeated and killed by Antiochus, also called Grypus ('Hooknose'), who went on to reign at Antioch from 125 to 96 BC. Hyrcanus was the son of Simon Maccabeus, who reigned in Jerusalem from 135 to 106 BC and often meddled in Syrian affairs during this time.

In the Year 200 BC

The opening quote of this poem comes from the inscription that Alexander the Great applied to the spoils that he won in battles with the Persian foe at Granicus (334 BC), Issus (333 BC) and Arbela (331 BC), the major victories that laid the foundation for the Hellenistic period. After Alexander's death his heirs divided his realm into three separate kingdoms, the Seleucid, the Macedonian and the Ptolemaic. An unnamed Greek is described by Cavafy as reading this inscription some 130 years after Alexander's victories, well aware of the historic consequences that these battles had for the Hellenization of so much of the known world. The Lacedaemonians alone had refused to send delegates to the congress at Corinth in 338 BC which elected Philip of Macedon (Alexander's father) head of the Greek confederacy.

In the Environs of Antioch

The Christians of Antioch buried their bishop, Babylas, in the grove of Apollo at Daphne, just outside of the city proper. The emperor Julian, who arrived in Antioch in AD 362 on his way to do battle with the Persians (where he would later be killed), insisted the body be removed. On the night the body was disinterred (22 October 362), the temple of Apollo (which Julian had just had restored) burnt down. Ammianus Marcellinus, the lieutenant and historiographer of Julian the Apostate, was an eyewitness to the event (*Res Gestae Libri* XXII.13.1). The scene is also described in Julian's own *Misopogon*.

Index of Titles

(Bold page numbers refer to the poems, non-bold numbers to the Notes.)

Index of First Lines

(Bold page numbers refer to the poems, non-bold numbers to the Notes.)

PENGUIN CLASSICS

THE MISANTHROPE AND OTHER PLAYS
MOLIÈRE

Such Foolish Affected Ladies/Tartuffe/The Misanthrope/The Doctor Despite
Himself/The Would-be Gentleman/Those Learned Ladies

'Let's not worry about the manners of the age and make more allowance for human
nature. Let's judge it less severely and look more kindly on its faults'

The six plays collected in this volume illustrate Molière's broad range of comic
devices, from satire and farce to slapstick and sophisticated wit and wordplay.
In *Tartuffe* and *The Doctor Despite Himself,* Molière shows us the foolishness of
those taken in by a religious hypocrite and a bogus physician, while *Such Foolish
Affected Ladies* and *Those Learned Ladies* are a humorous attack on the excessive
refinement and pedantry of the Parisian smart set. And in *The Misanthrope* and
The Would-Be Gentleman Molière warns us of the dangers of obsession and
intolerance. Exposing duplicity, mocking snobbery and revealing the horrors of
hypocrisy, Molière's plays are masterly studies in the absurdities of human nature.

All of the humour and panache of the original French has been preserved in John
Wood's translation. In his introduction, David Coward discusses the reception
each play received when it was first performed and how this has changed over the
centuries. This edition also includes a chronology, a bibliography and notes.

Translated by John Wood and David Coward with an introduction and notes by
David Coward

PENGUIN CLASSICS

OLD GORIOT
HONORÉ DE BALZAC

'His blue eyes, formerly so lively, seemed to have turned a sad leaden grey ...
People either pitied him or were shocked by him'

Monsieur Goriot is one of a select group of lodgers at Madame Vauquer's Parisian
boarding house. At first his wealth inspires respect, but as his circumstances are
reduced he becomes shunned by those around him, and soon his only remaining
visitors are two beautiful, mysterious young women. Goriot claims that they are his
daughters, but his fellow boarders, including master criminal Vautrin, have other
ideas. And when Eugene Rastignac, a poor but ambitious law student, learns the
truth, he decides to turn it to his advantage. *Old Goriot* is one of the key novels
of Balzac's Comèdie Humaine series, and a compelling examination of two
obsessions, love and money. Witty and brilliantly detailed, it is a superb study of
the bourgeoisie in the years following the French Revolution.

M. A. Crawford's fine translation is accompanied by an introduction discussing
Balzac's creation of distinctive characters from all levels of society, and his ability
to transform the lives of ordinary people into profound tragedy.

Translated with an introduction by M. A. Crawford

PENGUIN CLASSICS

LOVE AND MR LEWISHAM
H.G. WELLS

'He was no common Student, he was a man with a Secret Life'

Young, impoverished and ambitious, science student Mr Lewisham is locked in a struggle to further himself through academic achievement. But when his former sweetheart, Ethel Henderson, re-enters his life his strictly regimented existence is thrown into chaos by the resurgence of old passion. Driven by overwhelming desire, he pursues Ethel passionately, only to find that while she returns his love she also hides a dark secret. For she is involved in a plot of trickery that goes against his firmest beliefs, working as an assistant to her stepfather – a cynical charlatan 'mystic' who earns his living by deluding the weak-willed with sly trickery.

A biting critique on the spiritualist craze sweeping the nation, and a considered exploration of one man's conflict between love and ambition, *Love and Mr Lewisham* is the first of Wells's satires on social pretension in Edwardian England. Part of a brand new Penguin series of H. G. Wells's works, this edition includes a newly-established text, a full biographical essay on Wells, a further reading list and detailed notes.

Introduction by Gillian Beer
Textual Editing by Simon J. James
Notes by Simon J. James

Penguin Classics

THE LOST ESTATE (LE GRAND MEAULNES)
HENRI ALAIN-FOURNIER

'Meaulnes was everywhere, everything was filled with memories of our adolescence, now ended'

When Meaulnes first arrives at the local school in Sologne, everyone is captivated by his good looks, daring and charisma. But when he disappears for several days, and returns with tales of a strange party at a mysterious house and a beautiful girl hidden within it, Meaulnes has been changed forever. In his restless search for his Lost Estate and the happiness he found there, Meaulnes, observed by his loyal friend François, may risk losing everything he ever had. Poised between youthful admiration and adult resignation, Alain-Fournier's compelling narrator carries the reader through this evocative and often unbearably moving portrayal of desperate friendship and vanished adolescence.

Robin Buss's major new translation sensitively and accurately renders *Le Grand Meaulnes*'s poetically charged, expressive and deceptively simple style, while the introduction by *New Yorker* writer Adam Gopnik discusses the life of Alain-Fournier, who was killed in the First World War after writing this, his only novel.

'I find its depiction of a golden time and place just as poignant now' Nick Hornby

Translated by Robin Buss
With an introduction by Adam Gopnik

THE STORY OF PENGUIN CLASSICS

Before 1946 ... 'Classics' are mainly the domain of academics and students; readable editions for everyone else are almost unheard of. This all changes when a little-known classicist, E. V. Rieu, presents Penguin founder Allen Lane with the translation of Homer's *Odyssey* that he has been working on in his spare time.

1946 Penguin Classics debuts with *The Odyssey*, which promptly sells three million copies. Suddenly, classics are no longer for the privileged few.

1950s Rieu, now series editor, turns to professional writers for the best modern, readable translations, including Dorothy L. Sayers's *Inferno* and Robert Graves's unexpurgated *Twelve Caesars*.

1960s The Classics are given the distinctive black covers that have remained a constant throughout the life of the series. Rieu retires in 1964, hailing the Penguin Classics list as 'the greatest educative force of the twentieth century.'

1970s A new generation of translators swells the Penguin Classics ranks, introducing readers of English to classics of world literature from more than twenty languages. The list grows to encompass more history, philosophy, science, religion and politics.

1980s The Penguin American Library launches with titles such as *Uncle Tom's Cabin*, and joins forces with Penguin Classics to provide the most comprehensive library of world literature available from any paperback publisher.

1990s The launch of Penguin Audiobooks brings the classics to a listening audience for the first time, and in 1999 the worldwide launch of the Penguin Classics website extends their reach to the global online community.

The 21st Century Penguin Classics are completely redesigned for the first time in nearly twenty years. This world-famous series now consists of more than 1300 titles, making the widest range of the best books ever written available to millions – and constantly redefining what makes a 'classic'.

The Odyssey continues ...

The best books ever written

PENGUIN CLASSICS

SINCE 1946

Find out more at www.penguinclassics.com